PORTRAITS OF GREATNESS

General Editor
ENZO ORLANDI

Text by
GABRIELE MANDEL

Translator
MICHAEL CUNNINGHAM

Published 1970 by
THE HAMLYN PUBLISHING GROUP LTD
London · New York · Sydney · Toronto
Hamlyn House, The Centre, Feltham, Middlesex
SBN 600 33824 X
© 1968 Arnoldo Mondadori Editore
Translation © 1970 by
The Hamlyn Publishing Group Ltd
Printed in Italy by Arnoldo Mondadori, Verona

THE LIFE
AND
TIMES OF
GENGHIS KHAN

HAMLYN

London·New York·Sydney·Toronto

Below: This picture shows a Chinese sculpture of Genghis Khan seated upon his throne (Parma Museum, Italy). It is true to say that most representations of Genghis Khan which have survived the centuries are fairly reliable. When he was born he was originally given the name of 'Temujin' which means ironworker but the Chinese called him T'ie-mu-jen (the greatest man in the world). Chinggis Khan is the most accurate transliteration of his later name and this probably meant 'Lord of the Oceans'. However, there are numerous other ways of spelling his name and these include such variations as Jenghiz, Jinghis, Chinghiz and Chingiz. Genghis is one of the most common variants.

EMPEROR OF THE WORLD OR A PUNISHMENT FROM GOD?

'God in heaven; Khan of Khans, God's servant on earth. These are the orders of the Emperor of the World.' This was the seal of the man who was to be acclaimed Genghis Khan, 'Lord of the Oceans'; a man who controlled the largest empire the world has ever known, whose life altered the whole history of mankind and who was called 'the master of all the kings of the world', 'the mighty slayer of men' and 'the peerless, shining warrior'. Biographies which considered Genghis Khan in a favourable light were written by Rashid ed-Din Fadlullah in 1240, and by 'Ala ud-Din 'Ata-Malik Juvaini in 1257. There were other Persian writers, however, who reviled the Mongols and looked upon them as cruel and destructive, and Attila, king of the Huns, called Genghis 'a punishment from God'. Even today areas that had once been flourishing and prosperous – like the valley of the Bamyan, other parts of Afghanistan, Bukhara and the south of Samarkand – bear witness to the pillaging and destruction of the Mongol invaders. One man who admired Genghis, though, was Marco Polo and he wrote of him: 'Genghis Khan was a man of courage, wisdom and prudence . . . he used his power with insight and sound jugement.' Jacques de Vitry (1170-1240), who was Patriarch of Jerusalem, sent open letters from the Holy Land to the most powerful Christian kings. He told them about this new David 'who was of the Christian faith and came from India', who had defeated the King of Persia and was preparing to attack the Caliph so that he would be able to rebuild the walls of Jerusalem of gold and silver. All Europe rejoiced when it heard this news, but in vain, for within a short time Genghis was seen as the Gog who had been spoken of by the prophet Ezekiel. In an attempt to find out more about the new aggressors, Pope Innocent IV sent an Italian friar, Giovanni dal Piano dei Carpini (known in this country as Joannes de Plan Carpini) to Asia. His first impressions were the beginning of his famous account of the Mongols, *Historia mongolorum*: 'There are no cities or towns here, just an infertile, sandy terrain with no trees but particularly suitable as pasture ground for sheep and cattle. Everyone, including the emperor and his princes, cooks his own food and fires are made with dung . . . The climate is far from temperate.'

Left: These maps show from top to bottom the extent of the empire of Genghis Khan, Alexander the Great, Rome and Napoleon respectively. Genghis Khan's empire, which was the biggest the world has known, stretched from the Sea of Japan in the east to the mouth of the Danube in the west. No western conqueror did so much.

Above: an extract from Joannes de Plan Carpini's Historia mongolorum, *found in Turin and now in the Biblioteca Nazionale Universitaria. Soon after Genghis Khan's death, much information about the Mongols was obtained in Europe from ambassadors and missionaries; one of the most famous books was Marco Polo's* Il Milione, *a citizen of Venice.*

5

Right: This picture shows a large, Scythian bracelet which is made from gold (National Museum, Peshawar).
Below: This is a hat-pin which is made from silver, and on it can be seen representations of two imaginary animals who are worshipping the Dawn of Life. This is a characteristic design of Lur and Scythia.

Above: a detail from a silver vase which was made about the 11th century (National Museum, Budapest). This shows one of Attila's horsemen dragging a prisoner along by the hair. Right: a statuette of a wild goat (Facincani Collection, Milan). The statuette is made of silver and is typical of the art of the steppes which is produced in the region of the Ordos.

THE LAND OF THE FOUR DESERTS

From ancient times, a long, uncomfortable route had connected China with western Asia and Europe. Along this route Chinese silks and ceramics had come to be sold in the Mediterranean countries, whilst Buddhist monks, Roman merchants and dealers in Greek art had travelled to the legendary lands of the Orient. The more settled tribes who lived in the south soon began to hear of these splendid new civilisations from the many people that passed along this route, and as a result they modified their agriculture, adopted new art-forms and constructed magnificent temples and palaces. To the north of this route, joining east and west, lay the steppes and the land of the four deserts. It was a land of unending plains stretching from the China Sea to the lowlands of Hungary and was populated by wild, uncivilised tribes of nomads, hunters and peasants. For many centuries Scythians and Sarmatians had wandered through these lands, occasionally producing elementary decorative art – the only art to come from this enormous area at that time. However, the lives of these people were frequently disrupted by successive invasions of Huns, Avars, Tungusics, Turks, and finally, in the 12th century, by the Mongols under Genghis Khan. These invaders mainly occupied their time by tending livestock. They were also strikingly characterised by their destructive quarrels, by their poverty and resiliance to the cold. The Mongols were renowned as superb horsemen, exceptionally skilled with bows and arrows and were accustomed to riding for weeks on end in great discomfort which was only relieved by frenzied debauchery. They were small people and their eyes had become almond-shaped because of the wind, the dust and the blinding white of the snow. In winter they had to cover their tanned skin with a foul-smelling grease to protect them against the freezing temperatures. They hunted cattle and simply annihilated people that stood in their way. Civilised towns were plundered and devastated, and the inhabitants ruthlessly murdered, so that all marks of civilisation should be eliminated and the steppes return to their former 'dignity'. These tribesmen were the direct ancestors of the Magyars in Hungary, the Juan-juan in China and even some Amerindian tribes, and in one way and another helped to shape the future of Europe and Asia.

NOMADIC PEOPLES AND THE TRANSIENT EMPIRES OF CENTRAL ASIA

In the centuries preceding the Mongol Empire, the steppes of central Asia were racked by brutal, inter-tribal wars. One of the first tribes to dominate Asia was the Tochars, but their empire was short-lived as they were conquered by the Huns who were then overrun by the Toba in the 5th century. The Toba were then wiped out by the Tukius who were in turn defeated by the Uighurs. The Uighurs were literate, had an efficient bureaucracy and with their iron tools, built a capital, Kara Balghasun, and towns with stone houses and walls. Their empire lasted until the rise of the Kirgiz, who were soon conquered by the Khitai from China who built Peking as their capital. They were so powerful that the name of their dynasty has survived in several languages as the word for China (e.g. 'Cathay'). The Tartars, who lived in the vicinity of the River Amur, then joined the Sung, who lived in the south of China, in an attempt to drive the Khitai out; they succeeded in doing this but then came the Tungusic Jurchen who founded the Kin Dynasty. From Manchuria to the Altai Mountains and from the Great wall of China to the Arctic Circle was an immense area

peopled by Turks, Tartars, Naimans and Oirats who established large, but short-lived, empires. The Uighurs had migrated beyond the Altai after earlier reverses and, together with the Khara Khitai who lived in Persia, completed a vast mosaic of races who covered almost the whole of Asia. In the meantime, however, the Kirgiz, the Avars and the Huns were moving west and the Khitai, the Liao, the Kin and the Juan-juan were moving towards China. We know little of this period save that it was punctuated by battles and that most of the activity took place on a plain between the Orkhon and Lake Baikal, closed off to the east by the Kerulen. Here lived a Mongol tribe called the Kiyats who were surrounded by the Tartars and the Manchurians in the east, by the Merkits in the west, by the Taichut probably in the north and by the powerful confederacy of the Keraits in the south. The period was therefore one of instability, and this caused the Emperor Shih Huang Ti to construct the Great Wall of China in an unsuccessful attempt to protect his people from attack. Amalgamating several more ancient walls, it was eventually fifteen hundred miles long.

Facing page (above): a caravan in the Gobi Desert. Caravans composed of camels, yaks or horses are to this day the most efficient method of travelling in Mongolia. The gobi are large, rocky valleys which are characteristic of the desert and are full of hollows that are anything from six to a hundred yards wide. Below: Lake Baikal.

Top: a typical view of the desert terrain. In winter, the temperature can sink to 42° centigrade below zero and the Gobi is completely covered with ice. On the other hand, in summer, the temperature can rise to 38° centigrade and the desert is baked dry, so for most of the year nomads could only make very short journeys. They lived off their livestock and never thought of keeping hay or of cultivating the land. They accepted nature passively by never sowing the land, never owning anything and never protecting anything.
Centre: a group of Mongol children.

Left: a Mongol family in Thailand. The expansion of Genghis Khan's empire brought about a great deal of intermarriage between Mongols and local inhabitants. The most important Mongoloid peoples are the Siberians, the Tibetans, the Eskimoes and the Tungus. They came from the forests of the north, reared their families on the slopes of the great mountain ranges and later, either migrated onto the steppes or, alternatively, returned to their homeland. The Mongol is short and strong with short arms and legs, a long, flat face, well-tanned skin and slit eyes, adapted to the glare of sun and snow.

Below: this picture shows the baptism of a Mongol khan. Near right: two Nestorian talismans in gold, which depict the cross. Far right: two Nestorian talismans which are made of bronze representing a dove and the sun. Nestorianism was the official religion in Persia by the end of the 5th century and it eventually reached China in the 8th century. In the 12th and 13th centuries it had spread even further, and was widely adhered to by the Mongols. In Asia alone there were 200 Nestorian bishops and literally millions of adherents. It was crushed first by Tamberlane, then by the Kurds and more recently by the Turks, who attacked and massacred them.

A LINE OF FAMOUS KINGS AND HEROES

Far left: mosaic of a Nestorian. Middle left: a small bronze censer used by Manichaeans for making fires in. Near left: a ceramic of the T'ang Dynasty representing a Manichaean at prayer. Manichaeism was widespread among peoples as far apart as the Chinese, the Mongols and the southern Italians. Mongol kings were either Nestorian or Manichaean. Manichaeism was founded by Mani who lived from about 216 until about 276. He was born, some sources claim, of Persian parents, near the site of Baghdad and his religion contained a mixture of Persian and Christian elements. Mani called himself 'Mani the Apostle of Jesus Christ' and claimed that his predecessors had been Zoroaster, Hermes, Buddha and Plato.

One spring, a little over a thousand years ago, Borte Chinua (the grey-blue wolf) set up camp near the source of the Orkhon, upstream from Burkan Kaldun; here his wife, Gooa Maral (the fawn-coloured doe), had a son called Batachi. For twelve generations the pasture lands of Borte Chinua belonged to Dona, a giant with a single eye in the middle of his forehead, and to his brother Dobun Mergen (Dobun the Wise). One day a spirit from the skies visited Dobun's widow and she bore him three sons before he disappeared on a beam of the sun and the moon. The three sons were to be the first of three celebrated lines of warriors. One of these sons was Qaidu who was succeeded by Baiching Korchin, the awesome forefather of the Kiyats, Tumbinai the Cautious and Qabul Khan. Qabul wielded so much power that he was even respected by the Jurchen, who ruled the north of China, and he was able to assemble a large number of Mongol tribes to fight the Tartars and the Manchu. There is a tale in Mongol chronicles that Qabul pulled the Emperor's beard on a night of merry-making in Peking; there is little doubt that after fighting the Kin from 1135 to 1139 he won a famous victory and in consequence was able to impose a tribute of grain and livestock. On his death Qabul transferred his power, not to his son Kutula, but to Ambahai, leader of the Tarjuts and a collateral ancestor of Genghis Khan. Soon afterwards the Mongols became auxiliaries of the Kin Dynasty on what is now the Manchurian-Mongolian frontier but, with the help of an alliance with the Tartars, Ambahai continued to attack the Kin until he was finally defeated, captured and executed. His power passed to Kutula, whose brother Bartan the Brave was Genghis Khan's paternal grandfather. The Kin and the Tartars were beginning to destroy the seeds of Mongol unity once again, but they were opposed in this by a Kiyat chieftain called Yesugei, Bartan the Brave's son. It is thought that there were about 200,000 Mongols at this time, divided into some forty clans which were usually fighting with one another, and were only ever likely to obey a warrior who could prove his authority on the battlefield; Yesugei Ba'atur was just such a man. It is possible that he entered into an alliance at this time with Toghril, ruler of the mighty Keraits.

TEMUJIN'S UNSPOILT CHILDHOOD

One day Yesugei came across the caravan of a Merkit warrior. He was returning with his betrothed, Ö'elun, to his tribe, who had their camp to the north of the Keraits. Yesugei fell in love with the girl and, after a brief skirmish, killed the Merkit and carried her off to his own camp where she became his wife. In 1155 according to some Persian sources, and 1167 according to others, Ö'elun gave birth to her first child, a son. At that time, Yesugei was taking prisoners at the end of a victorious battle, and amongst them were two fierce Tartar chiefs, one of whom was called Temujin ögä. Yesugei decided to call his son Temujin as it was believed that the prowess of a defeated enemy was conferred on a newly-born child given the same name. The boy grew up according to the hard traditions of the steppes – in tents, on the open road, assailed on all sides by death, treachery and revenge. Children belonged to the lowest class amongst the Mongols; they competed with dogs for scraps from the tables (at which they were not allowed to sit), they fought amongst themselves, indeed they fought for survival itself. Their jobs were collecting dung – the only fuel known to the tribe – hunting rats and marmots, currying the horses and fishing. They went naked until the age of puberty, except for a felt coat which they wore on the march. Temujin had light golden skin, a low forehead, and his reddish-brown hair was arranged in two plaits that fell over his shoulders. He fought with his brothers and half-brothers, looked after the herds of cattle and practised shooting arrows; but more than anything else he listened to old tales and to the minstrels who sang of the legendary feats of his ancestors and of the dreams of a great, united Mongol race that was master of the steppes. One day when he was playing on the frozen River Onon with a friend called Jamukha, heir to the chieftainship of the Jajirat clan, he formed with this boy a pact of brotherhood which was to be of the greatest importance in the years to come. When Temujin was nine, Yesugei decided it was time to find a future wife for his son. In accordance with Mongol custom, the two left to visit the most distant clans; after travelling for many days they came to the camp of the Onggirats, a powerful tribe who were on friendly terms with the Kin, where they were the guests of the chieftain.

Shamanism was a religion followed by a great number of Mongols, including Genghis Khan, and by Eskimoes and Amerindians. The Shaman was doctor, priest and psychopompos by virtue of the fact that he could leave his body at will. His most important function was healing, and this he accomplished by finding out whether the sick man's soul had simply strayed from his village or been stolen by demons and imprisoned in another world. There were several stages of initiation, the last one involving dancing on crutches. By wearing a garment elaborately decorated with skins, and pieces of material, iron plaques and bells, and beating a drum until he lost consciousness, a fully-fledged Shaman communicated with the spirits and was able to foretell the future. He was the European equivalent of an African witchdoctor.

TEMUJIN'S LOVE GROWS FOR THE CHIEFTAIN'S FAIR DAUGHTER

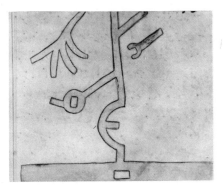

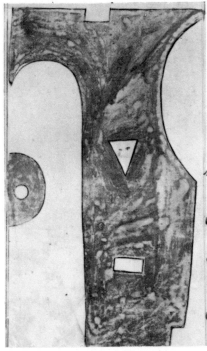

According to legend, Temujin fell in love with the chieftain's daughter, a reserved, serious-minded girl called Burte who was ten years old at the time. Other sources say that her father was so impressed by Temujin that he proposed the marriage himself. At all events, Yesugei probably saw that a union between his own clan and the Onggirats would be an advantageous one. Yesugei then gave the chieftain his own black stallion and left his son with him so that he should prove himself before being committed to marriage. It was a profitable stay for Temujin for he was able to learn about distant lands from Chinese merchants who visited the camp; he was also in a position to learn about city-life, weapons and the art of war. But the god of the Mongols was already shaping Temujin's destiny: one day, Munlik, one of Temujin's relatives, staggered into the camp, covered with perspiration and dust, and demanding Temujin's immediate return. It was not part of the agreement between Yesugei and the Onggirats that Temujin should leave so soon but the young man had displayed such signs of loyalty that the chieftain yielded. On the way back home, Munlik explained that Yesugei, while crossing the lands of the Tartars, had come across one of their clans holding a banquet; he had been welcomed as a friend and been seated at the top of the table and given the best food – an honour bestowed on anyone travelling over the steppes. But the Tartars, realising that he was an enemy, had given him poison to drink, and the great chieftain of the Kiyats had returned home and was now dying. When Temujin reached the camp his father was already dead. With him died the dream of a peaceful alliance of Mongols and of a strong, unified kingdom under one man.

Facing page: this photograph shows a Mongol Lamaist family at prayer. At one time central Asia had followed Buddhism in its original Indian form but it had been converted to a new religion based on exorcism and magic rites. Lamaism slowly grew in influence on the steppes finally ousting all other religions, and between 1570 and 1600 all Mongols were converted to it, although they were never able to shake off some of their old-established Shaman and Nestorian beliefs. Above (extreme left): Lamaist convent in China.

Note how stark is the scenery, and how the hills in the distance appear to be almost devoid of vegetation. Above: five illustrations from a history of the Mongols by Rashid ed-Din (Department of Oriental Manuscripts, Bibliothèque Nationale, Paris). Here we see history, war, transhumance (the seasonal movement of livestock from one region to another) and the interior of a Mongol tent, represented with an idealised symbolism which in numerous ways is strangely akin to contemporary abstract painting.

A PRINCE WITHOUT SUBJECTS AND HIS COURAGEOUS MOTHER

Below: these Chinese ceramic figures are representations of two warriors who came from outside the Great Wall of China; they are probably Tartars, a tribe which was so vast and powerful in the 12th century that other nomadic clans of the steppes, including the Mongols, used to call themselves by the same name. This fact was reported by Rashid ed-Din. For many years, even in Europe, the Mongols were inaccurately known as Tartars. The name Tartar originally came from Dada, or Tata, which was the name of a Mongolian tribe which in the 5th century used to inhabit what is now north-east Mongolia. The figures show the riding dress of a steppes warrior.

No sooner had the news of Yesugei's death been made known than all the chieftains loaded their carts, collected their cattle and left. Their subjects and slaves followed and all the entreaties of an elder to preserve unity under Yesugei's successor went for nothing; he was laughed at and physically attacked. To make matters worse, they made off with as much common property as they could lay their hands on. As a contemporary chronicler put it: 'The deep waters no longer flow, the mighty stone has crumbled'. After all, who in his right mind would kneel before a mere boy and obey his orders? Even the chieftains' oaths of allegiance were of no consequence. Each one wanted his own freedom and the opportunity to rule his clan as he pleased. Ö'elun, Yesugei's widow, then took the royal standard, which was decorated with the horn of a yak, and bravely went in search of those who had fled, and when she found them she harangued them for their folly. A few families returned but stayed for a short time only. The early spring of the following year saw Temujin, now head of his family, seated on his throne of white skins. He apparently had all the trappings of power though he was surrounded by women and children who were quite ready to try and survive on a diet of rats, squirrels and marmots, or even onions and radishes. Temujin's will never faltered, however, and his tiny band of followers slowly grew. Their hunting became more expert and successful, and they soon felt confident enough to ride into the lands of the Uringats and even into those of more dissident clans. These neighbours reacted with indifference or, at most, with curiosity, but news travels fast along the steppes and soon people realised that Temujin was becoming a forceful, strong, cunning and, above all, authoritarian chieftain. An example of this was when he killed a half-brother for stealing the spoils of the hunt. On this particular occasion, Ö'elun angrily denounced the act as that of a wolf or a mad dog biting its own self; a warrior had been killed and Yesugei's family would be wiped out if they could not keep peace amongst themselves. Also such thoughtless killings would make it impossible to take revenge on the unfaithful Taichuts who were allowing their cattle to graze on Kiyat land. All their strength must be directed towards this.

Left (top): a miniature which shows Ö'elun pursuing the clans that fled after Yesugei's death. This is an illustration from Rashid ed-Din's History of the World (Imperial Library, Tehran). (Centre): two miniature statues of seated yaks, which were both made by a craftsman of the steppes. (Bottom): a Tartar sword dama- scened with Lamaist deities. The Tartar warrior valued his horse and his weapons above everything else. Below: a Persian drawing of a Mongol warrior who is just on the point of drawing his sword. Note his round shield which he carries in his left hand and the bow slung over his shoulder. (Topkapi Saray Muzesi, Istanbul).

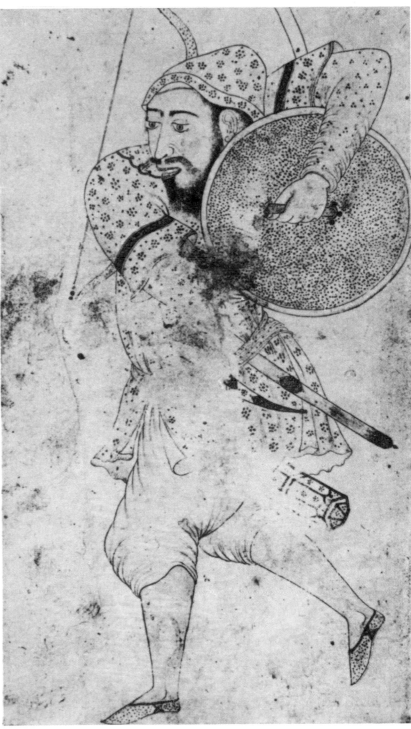

Below: the desert steppes were once the regular hunting-grounds of the Taichuts, who lived between the Onon and the Argun. Bottom: a wooden bowl which, according to a rather doubtful tradition, belonged to Genghis Khan as a young man (Lamaist convent near the town of Mandal Gobi).

Below: two convicts wearing a kanga, a type of wooden yoke that was a traditional form of punishment in Asia for hundreds of years. This photograph was taken in about 1905, at the time of the Boxer Rebellion. Bottom: a Persian miniature showing a prisoner-of-war wearing a kanga round his neck and wrists.

Before Genghis Khan became, by means of his brilliance and skill, the acknowledged leader of the Mongols, even when the majority of the tribes gave him allegiance, there were a number of occasions when he had to bow to superior forces and retreat. On one occasion, for example, he was in danger of being overwhelmed, and so he had to move his forces back for the sake of safety, to a marshy area where there was, unfortunately for himself and his men, no drinking water. However, Genghis Khan overcame this difficult problem with a simple solution, namely by straining the mud through linen bags, as is shown in this Persian miniature on the right. (Imperial Library, Tehran). He was accustomed to hardship. A childhood devoid of most comforts and bedevilled by wars, unrest and betrayals, no doubt, contributed substantially to Genghis Khan's strong and resourceful character.

TEMUJIN IS CAPTURED AND THEN ESCAPES

Even if Temujin's clan had been completely united, they would not have been able to withstand the might of Targutai, the leader of the Taichuts. It is probable that the Taichuts were in need of Temujin's royal standard, as well as his pasture grounds, because they had already assembled under their own flag most of the clans that had once been faithful to Yesugei. When Targutai decided that the time had come to incorporate Temujin's clan, he attacked their small camp but Temujin escaped to the mountains. On entering the camp, Targutai paid no attention to the tents or to Temujin's family who had stayed behind with the livestock and their few belongings; he was only after Temujin. Targutai took with him his best men, all trained at tracking down their enemy even on the hard, infertile terrain of the steppes. However, Temujin repeatedly outwitted his pursuers. After several days without food or drink, his senses became so dulled that he fell into a trap and was captured. With his neck and wrists tied to a *kanga* (a kind of yoke), he was taken to Targutai's camp where he was kept for a number of weeks. If he had died, one of his brothers would automatically have become king of the Kiyats; but Temujin was not one to give in easily. On the sixteenth day of the fourth moon of the spring, the Taichuts camped on the banks of the Onon to prepare for a feast. As a sign of their contempt for Temujin, they entrusted their prisoner to a young imbecile. In the middle of the night Temujin killed his watcher by striking him with the *kanga* and then hid in the river. Search-parties were organised, but though a member of the Saldus tribe, who was a guest of the Taichuts, saw Temujin, he did not give him away. When the search-parties moved outside the camp, Temujin ran to the tent of his new ally where his yoke was taken off him and immediately burnt on the fire. Experience had by now made Temujin more astute and cautious and he was able to slip past the guards and reach Burkan Kaldun, a mountain of great religious importance to the Mongols; here he made a sacrifice to the *Kengri* (the blue sky), sent for his family and followers, and procured two rams and fresh horses. Although suffering acute discomfort from his privation and constant vigilance, he now prepared for his revenge. His enemies would pay dearly for their insults.

19

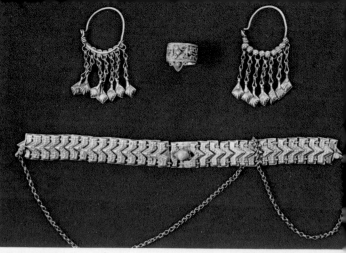

Near right: a Mongol woman wearing jewellery. Far right: jewellery worn by Nestorian wives in central Asia. Centre: coloured glass beads from Mongolistan. Persian money was adopted later in Mongol history. Bottom left: a Nepalese-Tibetan wife wearing Mongol jewellery. Bottom right: a Mongol necklace.

Genghis Khan's Codes of Law are interspersed with numerous comments such as this: 'Women may be foolish, flippant, unintelligent and disorderly, but this is because they have copied men. If a wife keeps her home well and takes pains to entertain guests, she will raise her husband's stock in their community. The wife is a sure indication of the husband's worth.' In time of war, women took over men's duties having to look after the cattle, keep the encampment tidy and administer their husbands' lands. They did nearly all the heavy work.

EIGHT HORSES FOR A WIFE

Below: two typical Mongolo-Tibetan necklaces which are made of metal and coral. Like all nomads, the Mongols were particularly expert goldsmiths and their specialities were filigree ornamentation, gold plaques, that were fixed onto their carts, and bronze symbols, which decorated their standards. Their swords were often engraved.

One day, while the Kiyats were either out hunting or with Remujin setting traps on the hills, a band of Taichuts plundered their little camp and stole eight of their nine horses. When Temujin returned he took the remaining horse, which had been used in the hunt, and set off in search of the attackers, travelling for three days with hardly a stop for food or rest. On the fourth day he came across Burgurtshi, a young man of the Arulat clan, who was guarding the horses; Burgurtshi recognised Temujin and, taking two of the horses and a bow, went with him. After avoiding the Taichuts for three days, they came to their encampment at dead of night and retrieved the remainder of the horses without being observed by the enemy. The next morning the Taichuts gave chase and soon caught them up, but Temujin and his companion decided not to stop and fight and frequently changed mounts so as to keep all the horses fresh. Stragglers began to appear among the pursuing Taichuts and Temujin, seeing his opportunity, killed their leader with his first arrow. When the second and then the third of the pursuers met the same end, the rest gave up the chase realising that they had met their match. Temujin and Burgurtshi then visited Naqu-bayan, Burgurtshi's father, who told them that their exploit was already on everybody's lips and implored the two young men to preserve their bond of brotherhood. Temujin reached his own camp, to find more followers were awaiting him; the sons of those who had been faithful to Yesugei and other fearless young men with a thirst for adventure, who had heard of Temujin's brilliant exploits, of his search for freedom and of his courage, and who now looked to him as their natural leader. So Temujin was at last able to organise small raids against the Taichuts, killing all but those who agreed to follow him. Furthermore, he was able to think in terms of at least returning to the Onggirats and marrying Burte who, he was quite sure, was still waiting for him.

Below: this photograph shows a Chinese wood-carving which represents a wedding-feast. Our information about weddings at the time of Genghis Khan is based in the main on contemporary Chinese annals. For example, during the time of the Yüan Dynasty many customs of the steppes were introduced into China.

Right: these two statues of Tara, represent a Lamaist goddess who was also the wife of the Tibetan king Sron-btsan-sgam-po. It was he who was responsible for converting the country to Buddhism. Here she is shown dressed in her wedding-garments whose style is strongly influenced by contemporary Mongol clothes.

FESTIVITIES AND FINE WEDDING PRESENTS

Below: Mongolo-Chinese statues of two ladies of Kublai's court, made of lacquered, painted and gilt earthenware some time during the Yüan Dynasty. Bottom: a painting of three Mongol ladies in wedding-dress (Musée Guimet, Paris). Joannes de Plan Carpini describes the wedding-garments of Mongol women thus: 'They wear a wide tunic down to the ground and a round head-dress of rushes or the barks of trees that is pointed at one end, squared-off at the other; on the top is a slender gold brooch made of silver or wood, or a plume sown to a veil that hangs down to the shoulders. Young women dress in a very similar style to men.' Felt was worn to keep out the cold.

Temujin arrived at the Onggirat camp with several gifts; these were not of any great value but had all been won in battle. He was given a hero's welcome, although the news of his exploits had rather overwhelmed Borte, who was waiting for him with considerable trepidation. Preparations for the wedding were begun and, in the middle of the hubbub and festivities, Temujin pretended to carry the girl off to some distant place, as was the custom of the Mongols. This was followed by the wedding-feast which lasted several days, after which Temujin and his wife departed. Temujin had countless splendid gifts, one of which – a black, sable cloak – was worth more than the rest of his belongings put together. He was accompanied by Burte and followed by servants, slaves, friends and a number of tents each mounted on a wooden cart. Realising that they were over-laden, Temujin gave away most of his presents; this included the sable cloak, which he gave to Toghril Khan, king of the Keraits, reminding him of the pact he had with Yesugei, according to which he was Temujin's godfather. Toghril responded by calling him his son and by giving him one of his men as a groom. Temujin was now able to avenge himself on Targutai with the help of Burte's father, Toghril, and Jamukha. He wanted to demonstrate his own courage and strength, but in a moment of over-confidence he gave the opportunity to a huge army of Merkits to attack the camp. They came from the forests of the frozen north and were the most barbarian of all the tribes. Twenty years before, Yesugei had robbed a Merkit warrior of his betrothed and the tribe were now seeking revenge. Temujin's men were caught unawares and they scattered and fled. When they returned they found the camp littered with corpses and the tents either in flames or empty. The greatest tragedy was that Burte, who had not been able to find a horse in the *mêlée*, had been captured by one of the Merkit chieftains and given to another chieftain to appease some other battle. Temujin neither despaired nor sought immediate revenge; he realised how rash he had been and climbed Burkan Kaldun, where he took off his belt and hat, went down on his right knee, and offered up fermented milk to the *Kengri* in thanksgiving for his own life being saved. Then he made plans to rescue his wife.

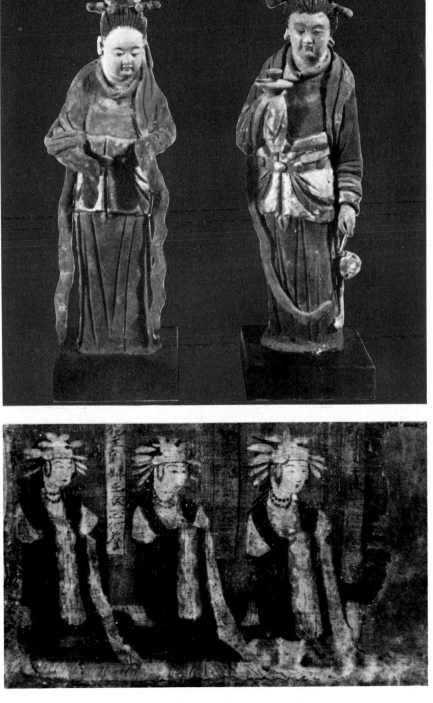

Below: a Chinese statue of a deified king, believed to be Toghril, King of the Keraits, the people who were Temujin's allies in his campaign to regain his stolen wife. Bottom: two statues representing Genghis Khan as a king of religious dogma (on the left) and king of war (on the right). The animistic beliefs of the east had all famous people transformed into deities, and later khans had no doubts whatever that they could achieve anything because they had God's sanction. It was plain to them that 'all lands' – all lands known to them – were subject to them, and while courteous in their reception of papal emissaries, dismissed their proselytizing with contempt.

TEMUJIN'S FRIENDS HELP TO FREE HIS WIFE

Temujin's army was at this time considerably strengthened by the addition of some of Toghril's soldiers as well as by a force of seasoned warriors from the numerous tribes that paid allegiance to Jamukha. These tribes had also once been faithful to Yesugei, the Mongol leader who had given Temujin his name. Jamukha himself was regarded by the tribesmen as one of the most important figures in the movement which saw the unification of the Mongols as the ultimate objective. This large combined force made Temujin its leader. He led them to the attack on a moonlit night, skilfully surrounding the Merkit camp and taking them by surprise. The enemy was completely routed; Temujin ran among the enemy tents shouting out his wife's name and he eventually found her with a new-born baby in her arms. This, his first son, he called Juchi (the Welcome One). Temujin was not interested in taking booty and would not let his troops pursue the enemy – his main object had been to find Burte. This was the first act of a new, visionary Temujin, a man who could see the foolhardiness of killing fugitive soldiers who might well become allies on some future occasion. During the feast on the banks of the Onon that followed this victory, minstrels sang of the 300 men who had died in the attack on Temujin's camp and of their womenfolk who were now the wives of Temujin's men. One of the elders recalled the time when all Mongols had been united and repeated the prophecies that a leader would come to them from heaven. After the feast, Toghril's soldiers left and Temujin and Jamukja travelled for a year and a half, speaking to all the chieftains, giving them presents and preparing for the day when all Mongols would be united. But all this was in the future; the great Khan had not yet entered history and much of the information we have is based on tradition. A collection of clan legends known as *The Secret History of the Mongols* is the principal source of information about the early life of Genghis Khan – or Temujin, the name by which he was known before he secured the allegiance of the wandering peoples of the central Asian table land. It was a historian of the conquered Persian nation, Juvaini, who recorded the career of the Mongol warrior in his *History of the World Conqueror,* an important medieval chronicle.

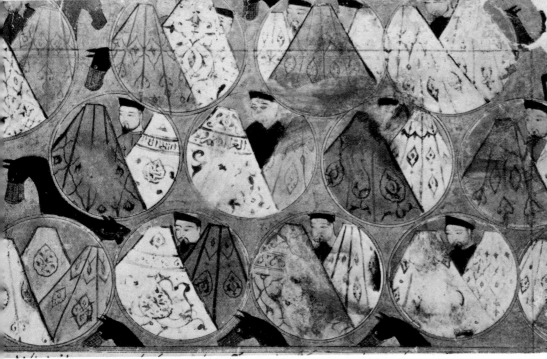

Above: a Mongolo-Turkish miniature showing Mongols on the march (Topkapi Saray Muzesi, Istanbul). Left: A Persian miniature which depicts an ordu *(Mongol encampment). The* ordu *was, in fact far from the cruel, ruthless band of men that the English derivation 'horde' might suggest; it was highly organised and strictly disciplined, and it only moved camp after scouts had discovered new grass-lands and watering-places that were suitable. Only then did the soldiers and cattle begin their journey with the tents carried on heavy carts drawn by oxen. There was even a rear-guard that gathered up any animals that had strayed and protected the caravan from the depredations of robbers. Mongol tents were put up by the women at each encampment.*

Right: a thirteenth-century painting of a Mongol horseman who lived during the Yüan Dynasty (Musée Guimet, Paris). The Mongols fought men and hunted animals in exactly the same way; their skill with bows and arrows was quite outstanding and they remained invincible until the invention of modern weapons such as rifles.

Above: a miniature showing the Mongols who are in the process of besieging a Persian city (Bibliothèque Nationale, Paris). Although the Mongols were unbeatable on the plains, they were less effective elsewhere and had to use Chinese and Persian prisoners to besiege walled towns. Right: Mongol horsemen resting in the desert (Topkapi Saray Muzesi, Istanbul). In this picture can be seen a quiver and the typical Mongol bow which had three curves.

26

HOW TEMUJIN BECAME GENGHIS KHAN

Below: this picture shows Mongol horsemen who are going forward in order to attack the enemy.
Bottom: Mongol horsemen during a siege. Genghis Khan methodically organised his troops. For example he divided his bowmen into brigades each with a hundred rows of men, and every row also consisting of a hundred men. This made for an ideal attacking force which was both effective and flexible and could easily manoeuvre to attack again if the lines were broken. The whole army was divided into three – the left, the centre and the right – and Genghis Khan always had a corps of trusted guards which was divided into the night guard and the day guard.

Temujin did not want to force his followers to make a choice between himself and Jamukha, nor did he want to upset his oldest friend and ally. So one night, on the advice of Burte and his mother, he rode out of the camp on his own. The response was immediate: he was followed by a clear majority of the clans. Some came because they saw him as the protector of the noblest traditions of the steppes, some because they saw him as their natural leader and some because they thought they could make use of him. There were soon 13,000 tents in Temujin's camp. He had already won the admiration of his men on many occasions because of his shrewdness, (as on the occasion when he had gone into a chieftain's tent and had been invited to sit down on the carpet but had refused because he had seen that the carpet concealed a large hole in the ground) and for his generosity (illustrated by the time when he had been riding up a hill and given his horse to a soldier who had no mount). In his camp, honours were bestowed according to rank and bravery, with the result that everyone was loyal to him and behaved in an orderly fashion. By his courageous feats he inspired the more blood-thirsty warriors and by his skill as a leader he gained the confidence of the wily chiefs of the older and more influential tribes. Temujin's diplomacy soon bore fruit when the chiefs assembled and unanimously conferred on him the title of Genghis Khan – Genghis coming from the Turkish *Tengiz* and Khan meaning 'prince' or 'leader'. They elected him their overall military leader and undertook to give him the best women and horses that they captured, and also to always go hunting under his leadership and offer him the best of the spoils. Finally they agreed that if they disobeyed his orders in war or in peace, he had the right to take all their belongings and if he wished abandon them in the middle of the desert. From that time on, Temujin began to organise his people by means of regulations and laws. He set up a private guard and a hierarchical system in the army as a whole, which was described by Joannes de Plan Carpini in 1248: 'The army is divided into groups of ten men, and each group is led by an officer; these officers are in turn grouped in tens and commanded by another officer, and so on.' His warriors were to obey his every order unhesitatingly.

27

Below: the banner of central Asia.
The Mongols fought under elaborate
insignia consisting of a long pole
decorated with horns and the tails
of horses or yaks, and at the very
top, the emblem of the tribe. Their
insignia, where the protective
spirit of the royal clan was believed
to live, were revered by the
Mongols.

AN ALLY OF THE CHINESE AGAINST THE TARTARS

Genghis Khan's abrupt rise to power incensed Jamukha as well as a life-long enemy, Targutai. The rift with Jamukha came about when one of his brothers stole one of Genghis Khan's horses only to be pursued and killed by their rightful owner; Jamukha then attacked but was forced to flee leaving only two of his lieutenants, whom he suspected later of having connived with the enemy. They too were put to death, and most of Jamukha's followers deserted to Genghis Khan's side. When 30,000 Taichuts led by Targutai attacked, Genghis Khan's army was prepared this time, but Genghis could see that not only were his forces too small, but that they were seriously hindered by tents and livestock. So he retreated and redisposed his camp in the form of a square, with a forest at the back, and the other three sides lined with soldiers, leaving the tents empty in the middle. When the enemy attacked again and threatened to overwhelm Genghis Khan's men, a small breach was made in one of the lines through which all his men escaped; the women had already retired into the forest taking with them the cattle and household goods. On entering the camp, the enemy, expecting to be able to pillage and take prisoners, instead found the tents empty. Shortly after this, Toghril was banished by his brother who had led a rebellion with the help of the Naimans. After unsuccessfully asking the Khara Khitai for help and waiting in vain for a contingent of Chinese soldiers requested by a loyal brother, he reached his godson's camp utterly exhausted and dying of hunger. Genghis welcomed Toghril, entertained him and his few men, and sent a message to the loyal brother that he should come at once. For two years they waited patiently for the right moment to take their revenge, and when it came they persuaded the loyal Keraits to revolt and the exiled king was once again allowed to sit on his throne. At this point, the Kin from the north of China sought an alliance with the Keraits so that the Tartars, who were threatening to control the entire eastern Gobi, should be surrounded by unfriendly forces. Ever faithful to Toghril, Genghis assembled all the clans that were loyal to him. The combined forces set off to take part in a campaign that was to culminate in a magnificent victory which further enhanced their leader's reputation.

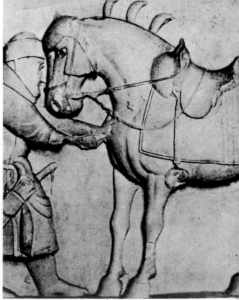

Above: a Mongolo-Turkish miniature showing a scene of nomadic life (University Library, Istanbul). Far left: a relief carving of a Tartar horseman under the T'ang Dynasty. Near left: a miniature depicting Genghis Khan fighting the Tartars (Bibliothèque Nationale, Paris). In about 1198 Toghril, King of the Keraits, and his vassal Genghis Khan supported the Kin in attacking the Tartars. They killed the Tartar leader and made off with a large quantity of booty. The Kin proclaimed Toghril wang (king) – a title he was hence-forth always known by – and Genghis was called ja'utquri (chieftain of the frontier guard).

Below: in this representation, Genghis Khan is shown seated upon his throne whilst he is surrounded by some of his numerous warriors. Right: these two miniatures depict the Mongols on the Caspian Sea and in Russia, where they fought under Gebe. They were essentially an inland people, who preferred the battlefield to the ocean.

Right: this photograph of a painting of Genghis Khan, shows the brilliant commander in battle. He is preceded by Gebe (Imperial Library, Tehran). Genghis Khan occasionally chose his generals from his personal guard but usually they came from amongst his personal friends. However, if he demonstrated great skill and acumen when he chose his generals, he was no less clever when he came to mastering the difficult and complicated arts of diplomacy. He was able, for example, to profit from his enemies' motives for waging war and thereby make his own interventions seem more legitimate.

GENGHIS PROMOTES A BOWMAN WHO WOUNDED HIM TO COMMANDER

The victory over the Tartars gave Genghis the pretext for further political manoeuvres and for ridding himself of dangerous pretenders to his throne. Genghis claimed that these rebels, which included some descendants of Qabul Khan, had disobeyed his call to participate in the war against the Tartars. He, therefore, defeated them in turn and put them to death. With Toghril's goodwill and help, Genghis then attacked the Naimans who, on the death of their king, were temporarily divided into factions. Unexpectedly Toghril asked for aid, saying that he was under pressure from a Naiman attack, and Genghis sent him troops commanded by his four bravest warriors. However, not for the first time, Toghril deceived him, and all of Genghis Khan's enemies were now united under Jamukha, whose ambition it was to rule all of Mongolia. In a final attempt to achieve this he gathered together all his followers on the banks of the Argun in 1201, and there proclaimed himself 'Emperor of the World'. At that time Genghis was fighting his erstwhile enemies, the Taichuts, and the outcome of the war was uncertain and still in some doubt, even though Targutai had been killed. Jamukha therefore felt that he could now attack Genghis, though he was let down by Toghril who insisted that he wanted to make a separate truce with Genghis. Then internal strife among his men prevented Jamukha from attacking in force. Shortly afterwards the balance tipped the other way, when Genghis was wounded in the neck by a Naiman arrow. One of his closest friends stayed up the whole night tending the wound to try and prevent it from festering. He then crawled into the enemy camp and stole some acid milk, which was considered to be the best medicine. By the following morning Genghis had made a miraculous recovery and managed to lead his troops into the battle that finally wiped out the Taichuts. Amongst the prisoners taken was the man who had so nearly killed Genghis; he stood before his captor and said that if he were killed his body would simply soil a small strip of ground, but if he were allowed to live then Genghis would have a good marksman who would help him conquer the world. Genghis made him one of his commanders and gave him the name of Gebe the Archer. It was the skill of this very man that helped Genghis to reach the Mediterranean.

Below left: a Chinese statue made under the T'ang Dynasty of a dromedary with two Siamese cats on its back. Unlike ordinary dromedaries, those from the northern deserts of the Gobi have long hair and short legs. Right: a caravan of dromedaries travelling along the steppes of northern China, just as they have done for centuries.

Ever since Genghis had begun to think of a united Mongol race, he had seen caravans of camels and dromedaries as a means of transporting merchandise and bringing back information on enemy movements. He was not slow to make use of this information – an early form of military intelligence. Camels carried the nomads' tents.

GENGHIS IMPOSES HIS WILL

The victory over the Naimans, the annihilation of the Taichuts and the dispersal of Jamukha's troops meant that Genghis no longer had anything to fear from the east, except that is the Tartars, who were the traditional enemies of the Mongols. Nearly every tribe of the central steppes had a debt to settle with the Tartars, and so there was no difficulty whatsoever in raising an enormous army, which was trained meticulously in accordance with Genghis Khan's elaborate instructions. Amonst Genghis Khan's detailed orders to the generals and chieftains, shortly before the battle commenced, was the prohibition of looting. All booty was to be gathered together and would be fairly distributed after the last battle. Genghis Khan likewise gave orders that every soldier who had to retreat must go back to his post as rapidly as possible. Any man who disobeyed this command would be beheaded. Genghis Khan's well-disciplined forces easily gained the upper hand over the disorganised enemy, and the Tartars were almost wiped out as a race. Genghis ordered all male prisoners who were taller than the hub of a cart to be executed. The rest were to be distributed amongst the tribes, and he himself married two Tartar princesses who had been captured from the enemy. Finally, much to the surprise of the nomadic tribes, he set about punishing those men on his own side who had disobeyed his orders. Amongst those who were disgraced were two rivals to his throne who were found to have booty; this was taken from them and shared out equally amongst the other chieftains. And so, Genghis Khan's iron will began to be felt amongst a people who had never previously accepted the laws or the authority of one leader. In fact, Genghis was the first man of this period to have clearly defined military and political aims, coupled with the ability to see them through. He was an outstanding leader.

Left: the Gobi Desert, the great waste which lies in the extreme south of Mongolia. Below: two photographs of the Caucasus Mountains (left) and the Pamirs (right). The large number of immense mountain ranges and the lack of fertile land have been the main reasons for Asian peoples remaining wandering nomads.

Below left and right: a Persian miniature depicting a Mongol hunt (Imperial Library, Tehran). Right: a Persian miniature showing Genghis on a hunt. Hunts were used by the Mongols as rehearsals for war. They were led by one of their chieftains who marked the area of the hunt by placing flags on the perimeter and deciding the spot where the hunt had to finish. Here the animals or birds that had been hunted were killed mercilessly, only a very small number being allowed to escape. According to an ancient custom, the fat of the first animal to be killed was rubbed on the middle finger of all the boys who had gone on a hunt for the first time.

GENGHIS GOES HUNTING

Below: a seventeenth-century European tapestry showing Genghis Khan on a hunt. Bottom: a Manchu fresco in Liao-Yang (Manchuria) of a hunting-scene, painted during the Han Dynasty (206BC–AD220). It is thought that Genghis Khan died of injuries following a fall from his horse whilst he was out hunting.

Among the Mongols, hunting was attended by considerable ritual. Genghis first gave a signal and a drum started beating; gamebirds, tigers, foxes, bears and young deer had been trapped by the noise of shouting and of horses' hooves in a circle that had relentlessly grown smaller and smaller every day. The camp almost seemed to be in a state of war – everybody carried arms, although they were forbidden to use them, messengers ran to and fro during the day, and a ring of sentries surrounded the prescribed area of the hunt at night to prevent the prey from escaping. On this, the last day, Genghis came to kill the first animal and afterwards the full-scale slaughter began. Only the last few survivors were allowed to escape, according to custom, and the success of the hunt was celebrated by a magnificent feast. The gaiety of one of these feasts on the first day of the fourth month of 1203 was overshadowed by bad news: Genghis had sent his fastest messenger to Toghril asking if his eldest son, Juchi, could marry a Kerait princess, but Toghril had refused. Meanwhile, Jamukha was hiding in Toghril's court and, at the same time, becoming close friends with his host's son. They were beginning to sow the seeds of dissension in Toghril's mind by saying that they were like skylarks nesting together in the same tree, while Genghis was a blood-thirsty bird of prey beyond their grasp. Toghril gave way to the entreaties of his son and his guest, and first tried to lure Genghis into a trap. This was unsuccessful and so he was obliged to attack openly, which he decided to do suddenly at the very moment that his messengers were arriving with conciliatory proposals. Two shepherds warned Genghis of the approaching army and he at once attacked it fiercely, throwing the enemy army into disarray while it was being put into battle-order. Genghis Khan's generals performed feats of astonishing bravery, one of them wounding Toghril's sons, another placing Genghis Khan's flag well behind the enemy lines while Ogadei, Genghis Khan's third son, slew an untold number of Keraits. On this occasion, however, the enemy's vast superiority of numbers was too great even for the bravery and discipline of Genghis Khan's men, and they were forced to make a strategic retreat under the cover of the night, escaping safely without losses.

Below: Il-khan miniature representing a warrior fighting a vision (Topkapi Saray Muzesi, Istanbul). The warrior is wearing the primitive armour typical of the Mongols, including a straight sword, replaced later by a scimitar. Bottom: Genghis Khan is here attacking a fortress (Bibliothèque Nationale, Paris).

Facing page (top): Genghis Khan's stirrups. They were handed down to his favourite grandson who gave them to his son-in-law Hetimandel Khan, in whose family they remained. (bottom left): Il-khan shield, helmet, arm-piece and axe. (bottom right): a Persian breastplate (Museo Poldi Pezzoli, Milan).

GENGHIS KHAN'S ENTREATY IS FOLLOWED BY WAR

'Toghril Khan, my godfather, why are you angry with me? Why do you frighten me so?... When you were a fugitive, did I not help you?... I shared my booty with you but I did not complain, and when your spoils were taken from you did my generals not hasten to make good your loss?... The first time you came to me you were riding a blind horse, you were dressed in rags and you were living on the meat of your last sheep – and I offered you all my lambs and horses... I am as close to you as the two wheels are to the cart: if one of the wheels breaks, the cart cannot continue...' These are extracts from a message that Genghis sent to Toghril; in fact he was oppressed by more serious problems since his situation had now become desperate and he needed to gain time. He had been abandoned by the less courageous tribes and had so few men and supplies that he was no longer able to resist outside attacks. To escape, he travelled enormous distances to the north of Manchuria where he spent the winter of 1203 obtaining new weapons for his army, warning allies, and establishing diplomatic relations with distant Moslem traders. Genghis then sent one of his generals to spy on Toghril. The general told the Kerait king that he had searched everywhere but had not been able to find Genghis; if Toghril could tell him where Genghis was, he would persuade the Mongol to surrender. Toghril gave the general a scout so that he could track down their enemy. Meanwhile, Genghis was advancing with his troops, making new allies and keeping himself informed about the movements of his enemies. Toghril was so confident of both Genghis Khan's weakness and his unwillingness to wage war, that he plundered the encampments of his Mongol allies. He was celebrating by holding a feast when Genghis suddenly attacked. The battle was fierce but the Keraits were forced to surrender after three days. The Kerait general was captured and pleaded that he had protracted the fight so that his king might escape; if it was Genghis Khan's will he would die honourably, but if he was allowed to live he would serve him bravely. Genghis at once made him captain of his night guard, but soon afterwards Toghril was put to death by the revengeful Naimans, to whose lands he had fled in order to re-equip himself and his men and the feud was at an end.

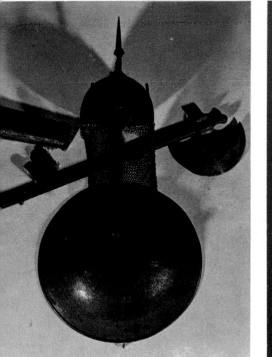

Joannes de Plan Carpini described Mongol weapons and armour thus: 'All Mongol warriors have two or three bows . . . three large quivers filled with arrows, an axe, rope . . . The more prosperous have swords that are extremely sharp and slightly curved, and armour to protect their horses, including the legs; all have helmets and breast-plates . . . The breast-plate consists of at least five pieces . . . the top of the helmet is made of iron and iron mesh, but the circular part that protects the neck and face is made of hide . . . Some warriors have a lance with a hook at the end for unsaddling the enemy.' They also had arrows of varying sizes, with points sharpened with a file, and shields made of lacquered wicker or hide.

Near right: an Indian miniature of a dromedary lost in the desert (Central Museum, Lahore). Far right: a carrion in the Gobi Desert. At noon, the heat will fry an egg. Below: a stone venerated by the Mongols because it resembled Burkan Kaldun in shape. This is a typical example of the combination of Animism and artistic taste.

GENGHIS KHAN'S WHITE FLAG FLIES OVER A UNITED MONGOL EMPIRE

Genghis was now threatened on only two fronts: in the south by the Onguts, and in the west by the Naimans. At that time the Naimen were harbouring Jamukha and the remnants of various tribes, including a few Tartars and Keraits who had escaped being massacred by the Mongols. The Naiman king was persuaded by his guests to attack Genghis Khan and ally with the Onguts. Alaqushi, the king of the Onguts, agreed to the conditions of the alliance but before doing so informed Genghis. Genghis had just spent the winter of 1203-1204 refitting his camp, and his horses and men were unfit. 'When the tiger is licking its wounds it is in no mood for fighting' says a Mongol proverb, but the 'tiger' called a meeting of his generals and they agreed to go to war. The army opposing them consisted of 80,000 trained, armed and disciplined men, for the Naimans had adopted laws, writing and administrative skills from their Uighur neighbours. Genghis put into his vanguard his thinnest soldiers, lightly armed and mounted on his weakest horses; this was a trick to lure the enemy into attacking without taking proper precautions. The Naimans had in fact taken up a position near a mountain so that they had an easy escape route if they needed one, but when they saw Genghis Khan's emaciated troops they attacked at once and promptly fell into the trap. That evening, the Naiman king looked down from the top of the hill, where he was dying, to see his few surviving warriors being pursued and slaughtered by Genghis Khan's men; he may well have thought of Jamukha who had fled as soon as the battle had begun to go against him and of his other friends who had done likewise. Genghis then defeated the Merkits who at once offered to fight henceforth for the Mongols. Genghis accepted this offer and, as a sign of friendship, married a Merkit girl famed for her beauty. A few pockets of resistance were still being formed by the Naimans and Merkits, but Genghis soon put an end to this. When Jamukha was captured he was executed by strangling; Jamukha had been sent to Genghis by his own men and they too were executed for their betrayal. Other clans, like the Kirgiz and the Oirats, submitted voluntarily to Genghis Khan's power and for the first time his white standard flew over a united Mongol empire.

FOREIGNERS ARE IMPRESSED BY GENGHIS KHAN'S LAWS

In 1206, the Year of the Panther, Genghis summoned a *quriltai* (an assembly of Mongol chieftains) at which he was solemnly proclaimed 'Lord of all who live in tents'. His power now extended for 1,000 miles from the Great Wall of China to the Tarbagatay Mountains and for 700 miles from the Gobi Desert to Siberia. About thirty-two tribes gave allegiance to him and he divided them into three large groups: those of the centre, those on the left and those on the right – in exactly the same way as he arranged his forces in battle-order. A traditionally rigid system of class-distinction was strictly adhered to; the classes in descending order were: Genghis Khan's own family or the *Altan Uruk* (the Golden Family), the khans or princes (*noyan* or *wang*), the free nobles (*arat*), the nobles (*taiji*), the citizens (*nökud*) and the slaves (*unaghan*). The bureaucracy was soon purged of Shamanism and Genghis entrusted general administration and education to Tata Tonga, an Uighur, and to the post of supreme judge he appointed one of his adopted sons. The laws (*yasa*) and the punishment (*biliq*) covered everything imaginable, including such simple things as caring for the horses' legs and sharing the spoils of the hunt; all these laws carried Genghis Khan's seal of approval, and everyone from Genghis down to the most humble slave observed them. Thanks to this system, the whole empire was ruled with a sense of justice that inspired the admiration of visitors such as Joannes de Plan Caprini, Odocrico da Pordenone (1265?-1331), William de Rubruquis (1215-1295) and Marco Polo. Regrettably, no text of these laws has survived to the present day, and we cannot rely on the extracts that have been passed down by word of mouth to succeeding generations.

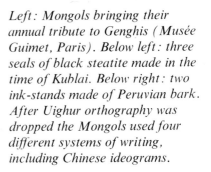

Left: Mongols bringing their annual tribute to Genghis (Musée Guimet, Paris). Below left: three seals of black steatite made in the time of Kublai. Below right: two ink-stands made of Peruvian bark. After Uighur orthography was dropped the Mongols used four different systems of writing, including Chinese ideograms.

Throughout the term of his leadership of the Mongol people Genghis issued Yasa (laws) and Biliq (punishments), and continued to do so until the day of his death. Of his numerous commands two were: 'All chieftains and warriors must scrupulously obey these laws or the Mongol state will be too weak to survive' and 'If the kings who reign 500 years, 1,000 years, 10,000 years after me leave these laws exactly as they stand, the Mongol state will remain powerful.' There is no doubt that these laws contributed substantially to the unification of the Mongols, who had never had such a system.

*Below: a Kin soldier. The Kin, or Jurchen, were a Tungusic race from the north who conquered northern China in about 1123.
Right: part of the Great Wall of China, built by Shih Huang Ti and finished in 214 BC; it is 1,500 miles long and is sometimes as much as nine yards wide. It is said it would be visible from the moon.*

Near right: a Mongol warrior; this illustration is taken from an old Chinese encyclopedia. Middle right: two Mongol horsemen. Far right: a statue of a Kitan bowman made during the T'ang Dynasty. Genghis Khan's army in China is described by Juvaini in these words: 'The flashing of the weapons in the sun and the tremendous noise of the horses made the desert look like a storm-tossed ocean, so immense that it was impossible to see the centre or the banks.' The Persian historian was writing after the event, but what is known of the full force of a Mongol attack bears out his vivid description. Mongol horses were extraordinary agile, and could obey orders just like trained dogs.

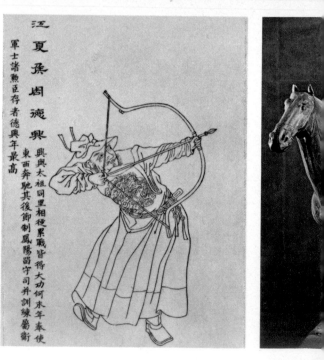

A VAST ARMY MARCHES ON CHINA

In the spring of the year 1211, Genghis Khan gathered his soldiers together and, in front of 200,000 of them invoking the *Kengri*, prayed for assistance from the god of the Mongols in the forthcoming battles. He then proceeded to fast for three days and nights, before starting off on his march. He did not take with him on this journey any baggage-train since he had brought along his own livestock and, besides, there were always numerous enemy towns and villages which could be plundered along the way. The enormous army crossed the Gobi Desert just as the thaw began and the snows of winter were beginning to melt, and when it eventually reached the border of the Kin Empire the scene was already set for one of the most extraordinary exploits in the history of mankind. Genghis Khan's success was made possible because of a number of factors. In the first place Genghis had previously sworn to be loyal to the Emperor of China, but he was now dead and, as a result, his place had been taken by his ineffectual, faint-hearted and unwarlike son, who was soon assassinated by a treacherous minister. Secondly, Genghis had successfully tried out his forces on the field of battle in a campaign against the Hsi Hsia. These people, who lived in Kansu and Ningsia-Hui in the north-west of China, he had succeeded in defeating in 1209. Thirdly, Genghis had secured the complicity of the Turkish Onguts who lived in the vicinity of a long section of the Great Wall, and with their help purchased the good-will of some Chinese garrisons that guarded the Wall. It was thus easy for the Mongols to gain entry into China where they were at last able to avenge long-standing wrongs by cruelly executing the Chinese leaders and the Liao, who were related to the Mongols. Genghis then put the legitimate heir on to the throne, thereby ensuring his loyalty and goodwill and rendering the north-east frontier with China quite harmless. The garrisons of the Chinese hinterland were next in line for attack, and four Chinese armies were defeated in a single battle; this was achieved by diverting rivers and by the use of siege machines, hitherto never used on the steppes. Genghis then divided his army in three and ordered them to conquer as much of the Kin Dynasty as they could and then join up at the walls of Peking with all their booty.

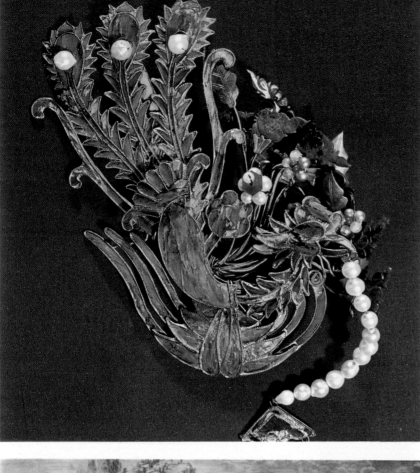

PEKING FALLS AND THE TRENCHES AROUND THE CITY WALLS ARE FILLED WITH BLOOD

Genghis Khan's men, who were utterly exhausted after so much fighting, and were also seriously hampered by the large quantities of booty which they were carrying, were unexpectedly attacked by Kin warriors, and they would have been defeated if reinforcements led by a Kin general from the south had managed to arrive in time. Fortunately for Genghis, the Kin were obliged to return to the city, where they were soon completely routed. When the forces from the south eventually arrived, they in their turn were defeated, although they were able to reach the city and behead the minister who had had the previous emperor murdered. China was thus deprived of a true, if somewhat ruthless patriot, and the treaty agreed to by his heir with Genghis cost him his entire fortune. When Genghis Khan eventually took leave of Peking he also took with him a wife from the Imperial House of China and a dowry which consisted of an immense booty, as well as untold thousands of prisoners. However, it was now summer and, clearly, the weather was quite unsuitable for crossing the Gobi Desert, so Genghis Khan decided on a simple expedient for ridding himself of the burden of his prisoners. He had them all beheaded. He then sent out emissaries to try and establish some kind of diplomatic relationship with the kingdom in the south of China, which was ruled by the Sung Dynasty. However, the new emperor in Peking was suspicious, and read danger into this new move of Genghis Khan. He decided, therefore, to move his capital to Pien-ching (modern K'ai-feng), but Genghis considered that their pact had thereby been broken and destroyed Peking.

Top: a piece of jewellery that belonged to the last Empress of China of the Manchu dynasty who called themselves the Ch'ing. It is in the shape of a humming-bird and is made of silver, gold, precious stones and pearls. It was the Mongols who introduced the Chinese to elaborate jewellery of such brilliant craftsmanship.
Above: an engraving of a battle between the Mongols and Chinese by the Jesuit, Giuseppe Castiglione.
Above right: an Il-khan miniature showing a princess in a garden.
Facing page: a Persian miniature showing Genghis on his throne.

After Peking was taken, a prisoner was brought to Genghis – Yeh-lü Ch'u-ts'ai. Genghis reminded him that the Kin had been the Kitans' most hated enemy but now the Mongols had conquered his people. Yeh-lü Ch'u-ts'ai answered that his family had always been faithful subjects of the Kin and that he would feel it dishonest and hypocritical to say that he hated the Kin emperor; such loyalty pleased Genghis and the Kitan was made his closest adviser and later became one of the most astute ministers Asia has ever known. He lived from 1190 to 1244.

GENGHIS KHAN MARCHES INTO PERSIA

When Genghis returned to northern China, a Naiman, who in fact was an old enemy of his, married a daughter of the king of the Khara Khitai, among whom he had sought refuge. He managed to get rid of his father-in-law, with the assistance of the Shah of Khorezm, and was then able to take over control of the entire kingdom. Afterwards the Naimai was persuaded by his Buddhist wife to persecute all Moslems in his territory. Unfortunately, amongst the people he killed was a chieftain of a neighbouring tribe, who was also a vassal of Genghis Khan. In 1218 Gebe was ordered to march on this Naiman prince with an army of 20,000 men and restore the Moslem religion. The Moslems welcomed the Mongols as liberators and joined with them in putting the Naimans to flight. They finally killed their own prince on the slopes of the Pamirs. In accordance with Genghis Khan's express orders, his men did not carry off any booty, unlike the army of the Shah of Khorezm which had mercilessly plundered all Moslem encampments. With the annexation of the kingdom of the Khara Khitai, a territory which was as large as Mongolia itself, Genghis Khan's empire now bordered on one of the most civilised and historic areas in the world: the Moslem strongholds of Persia and Afghanistan. For all his ambition and authority, the Shah of Persia, 'Ala ud-Din Mohammed, was not in complete control of the situation. He had alienated many of his subjects and was at that time preparing to march on Baghdad to depose the Caliph. Genghis attempted to form diplomatic and commercial treaties with the Shah, receiving envoys and caravans of merchants and in turn sending back to a caravan of ambassadors.

Top left: Il-khan miniature of a prince, grooms and horses (British Museum, London). Top right: Chinese painting of the Yüan Dynasty showing a Mongol horse drinking (Musée Guimet, Paris). Above: a Mongolo-Chinese incense-burner. Facing page (top): Chinese painting of the Yüan Dynasty depicting a Mongol groom with three horses. (bottom): a Chinese painting of one of Genghis Khan's princes (formerly in the Imperial Palace, Peking).

Horses probably originally came from Mongolia and were then brought to the west by merchants. Joannes de Plan Carpini wrote: 'Both men and women spend extremely long periods on horseback and take very great care of their horses . . . After a horse has been ridden for a day it rests for three or four; as the Mongols have so many horses there is no need to tire them out. They do not eat straw or hay . . . in winter they are able to find grass under the snow.'

GENGHIS ANNIHILATES THE PERSIAN FORCES

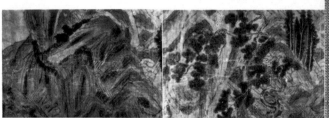

A diplomatic and cultural mission which had been sent by Genghis Khan travelled as far as Otrar, but then it was attacked by the local governor's troops and all the envoys were killed. Genghis demanded that he should receive some form of compensation for this hostile act. However, when this was refused by the Shah, he mobilised his army and sent a message to the Persian court saying that the Shah had chosen war instead of friendship; God alone could tell the outcome, but just as there could not be two suns in the sky, so there could not be two emperors on earth. He assembled about 200,000 men on the shores of Lake Baikal and told them of the man who had so little respect for the Khan of the Mongols. He also promised that every soldier who obeyed his orders would receive a share of the booty. On the other hand, those who disobeyed would be punished, together with their wives and children. Then, leaving Mongolia in the care of one of his brothers, Genghis Khan led his army off on one of the most arduous journeys ever undertaken – for it went over deserts, plains and mountain ranges that included the Himalayas. In the autumn of 1219 they finally reached Otrar, where the envoys had been put to death and the fortress was overrun by Jagatai and Ogadei, who were two of Genghis Khan's sons. Frontier garrisons were the next to be devastated, and in February 1220 Bukhara was besieged. The city had been abandoned by its garrison and was promptly evacuated of those who were still living there, whereupon it was sacked by the Mongols and set on fire. The next place to be conquered was Samarkand, which was set on fire by incendiaries propelled over the walls by catapults; the trenches by the walls were then filled with the prisoners from Bukhara, who were shot dead with arrows. Samarkand was vigorously defended, but it eventually capitulated and the entire population was executed. Meanwhile the Shah had fled.

At the head of the text and below : scroll depicting Genghis Khan visiting a group of engineers diverting a river. On the right of the facing page, and at the bottom of this, are two details of this scroll. Genghis can be seen holding the banner with nine tails. This scroll was formerly in the Imperial Palace, Peking.

Up to the time when China was conquered, Genghis was unaware of the existence of siege machines, but when he attacked Persia he had with him some Chinese engineers who built one in the course of the campaign against Shah 'Ala ud-Din. Before gunpowder was used in Europe, Genghis Khan's Chinese engineers developed naptha flame-throwers and a sort of gun that set wooden defences on fire. Another fighting technique was the use of catapults, which the Mongols copied from the Moslems. However, the Mongols' greatest exploits were achieved by diverting rivers and thereby flooding a city or causing its inhabitants to die of thirst.

Below: an Asian tapestry representing Genghis Khan (Alexander the Great, according to some sources) on a hunt. Bottom: a stone relief depicting warriors of the Hindu Kush ready for war (National Museum, Pakistan). Mongol advances brought about radical ethnic changes, particularly in the area now known as Pakistan which was part of the familiar way west through Afghanistan to Persia. The frequent massacres in Persia and Afghanistan – although not comparable with Tamberlane's pyramids of living bodies covered with mortar and bricks – almost caused some tribes, like the Kafirs, to die out. Many young Asian civilisations also disappeared.

GENGHIS KHAN PROCLAIMS HIMSELF AN ALLY OF THE GRAND SULTAN

Shah Mohammed fled first to Khurasan and thence to the towns of Nishapur and Kazvin, the latter being in unfriendly territory. Gebe and Subutai were following close behind, destroying any city that stood in their way – Tus, Damghan, Semnan, Ray (a town famous for its ceramics, where not one person survived the onslaught save for the hundred or so Mongol craftsmen who had been living there as slaves), Zenjan and Kazvin. By the time the Shah reached Hamadan all his soldiers had been killed, and he was obliged to take refuge on an island in the Caspian Sea where he died alone in the most squalid surroundings in the autumn of 1220. Gebe and Subutai continued their campaign in the west, having sent news of the Shah's death to Genghis, who was spending the winter at an encampment on the banks of the Amu-Dar'ya. Later, when the armies of Juchi, Jagatai and Ogadei arrived, they besieged the city of Gurgan, capital of Khorezm. To reach the city, which had been built on an island, long-range, heavy catapults were used to send containers of burning pitch over the walls, and experiments were made with armoured boats. The general of the forces defending Gurgan, Timur Malik, put up a heroic resistance, but the city was eventually taken. Nearly all the inhabitants had been killed during the fighting, and those that survived were killed as they emerged from their hiding-places by the Mongols returning to set fire to the defeated city. A similar fate befell Herat, where there were only sixteen survivors, and Transoxiana, which was part of Khurasan at that time and was overrun by Tului, Genghis Khan's fourth and youngest son. Tului also captured the town of Merv. Afterwards, seated on a throne made entirely of gold, he watched while the right ears and heads of all the inhabitants were piled up in front of him; the only people allowed to survive were four hundred craftsmen. At Nishapur, a town noted for its ceramics, even the corpses were beheaded, for the Mongols believed that their enemy might be able somehow to come back to life. Elsewhere many outstanding pieces of Persian architecture were destroyed, like the tomb and mausoleum of Harun al-Rashid as well as some 2,000 mosques – all raised to the ground on the orders of a man who had called himself an ally of the Grand Sultan and a defender of the Moslem faith.

Left: a Mongol funeral statue carved in wood of two stylized horses, one being ridden by a warrior. The statue was made in Afghanistan. Below: a very rudimentary stone sculpture thought to have been made by a Mongol craftsman but more probably by a Seljuk. Bottom: a sculpture of a warrior from central Kafiristan.

Right: ruins of fortresses in Afghanistan (near right) and the Hindu Kush (far right) destroyed by Genghis. Below: Chinese painting of the Yüan Dynasty showing Genghis Khan hunting. Facing page (top): Genghis talking from a pulpit in Bukhara. (Bottom): a photograph of Mogol in Mongolia today.

52

GENGHIS KHAN PURSUES THE SHAH'S SON TO THE BANKS OF THE INDUS

It was characteristic of Genghis Khan's boldness and military genius to take great pains to find out about the Persian political situation and the strength of its army before setting out to conquer Persia (present-day Iran, Iraq, Afghanistan and part of Russia). Conversely, Shah 'Ala ud-Din knew nothing of Mongolia and did not believe that an army could travel so far over deserts and mountains. Persian civilisation was destroyed by the amazing and intricate Mongol system of routes, caravans, resting-places and messengers, which allowed them to cover vast distances. Mongol generals travelled with as many as eighteen horses, in order always to have a fresh mount.

After conquering Persia, Genghis was faced by one of his most feared adversaries – Afghanistan. This tiny mountain country had known moments of glory, (as when it had conquered India and Persia), but it was now in a state of political upheavel. Shah Mohammed's son, Jalal ed-Din, had taken refuge at Ghazni, the scene of innumerable brave feats and of many Afghan revolts, and was raising an army there. After destroying the city of Thaleqan, Genghis was joined by the armies of Jagatai and Ogadei. He then crossed the Hindu Kush and attacked the Afghan garrison at Bamyan. In the course of the bitter siege, Jagatai's son was killed; Genghis honoured him with a magnificent funeral and then returned to the attack of Bamyan, this time easily overruning the town; he forbade his men to carry off any booty, but they destroyed every living thing – men, animals, birds, and even insects and vegetation. Genghis next detached some of his forces and sent them to attack Jalal ed-Din, who was now in Kabul. The Mongols were commanded by a prince who was only fifteen years old and who had until then only hunted reindeer on the ice at night. He took on the celebrated warrior north of Kabul and lost; this was the only major defeat Genghis Khan's armies are known to have incurred. When Genghis heard of the disaster, he was not angry; he merely said that victories had hitherto come too easily to his youthful general but from now on the boy would take greater care. Genghis then went to the scene of the defeat and took stock of the situation. He laid siege to Ghazni, cutting off all lines of communication with the south of Afghanistan. Soon afterwards he set off in pursuit of the enemy armies, eventually catching up with them on the banks of the Indus on November 24th, 1221. Jalal ed-Din was hemmed in by Genghis Khan's army on three sides and by the river behind him and, despite his stout resistance, the prince was utterly routed by the Mongols' methodical attacks and wheeling movements. Jalal ingeniously passed through the Mongol lines and managed to cross the river and reach Delhi, where he left his wives and fortune. The Mongols followed him into India but were forced by the intense heat to turn back, sacking the towns of Peshawar, Lahore and Multan on the way.

GENGHIS KHAN TYRANNISES THE PEOPLE OF PERSIA AND AFGHANISTAN

On one occasion in Khorezm, Genghis is said to have been opposed by a larger and better equipped army belonging to the Shah, although he had with him over 200,000 men. The Shah, however, divided his army into three, thereby weakening his position and, at the same time, he alienated his generals and allied princes by his arrogance. These weak points were all that Genghis needed to overpower his enemy; the information he gathered on the enemy's movements, his elaborate preparations and the speed of his horsemen did the rest. As a result, most of Persia's fertile land was devastated and the irrigation canals rendered useless. Gardens and orchards were contaminated with the stench of fires and corpses, and in the ravaged cities not a thing moved, for even the dogs and rats had been killed. Perhaps the Persians were too civilised, and pacific and thus presented a tempting prey for the barbaric invaders from the steppes. The actions of the Mongols here in Persia were in direct contrast to their innate pride in 'the nobility of the steppes', for elsewhere they had administered their newly conquered lands in exemplary fashion. Then a Persian city was to be attacked, all the inhabitants of the surrounding countryside were made prisoners, dressed in Mongol clothes, and sent on horseback to the besieged city to give the impression of an immense Mongol force – each of Genghis Khan's men had come to Persia with five horses so there were always plenty of spare mounts. Sometimes these prisoners took their places in the van, either to act as a human shield for the Mongols, to fill up the trenches in front of the city walls or to form a human ramp up to the top of the walls. It was normal, however, for the prisoners to be beheaded – methodically and in cold blood; the execution of the population of Merv lasted a whole week. Thus Persia and Afghanistan were ravaged and their people annihilated. Genghis Khan's opposition to the Moslem religion was based quite simply on the fact that ritual ablutions were compulsory under Mohammedan law, while Mongols washed neither their bodies nor their clothes in running water, and bathing was considered by them as a sign of weakness. In consequence, the glories of Persian civilisation were wiped out and the advance of Islam was seriously hindered.

The Mongol conquest of Persia consisted of one long series of massacres, according to Moslem sources and Joannes de Plan Carpini: 'The Mongols killed all prisoners that were not needed as slaves; the victims were shared among the Mongol officers and ten were given to each soldier to be executed with a two-edged axe.' According to the great Venetian traveller, Marco Polo, however, a rather different situation prevailed: 'In an extremely short space of time, Genghis Khan conquered eight provinces and neither plundered nor robbed . . . All the conquered nations and races joyfully proclaimed him their leader and praised him for his goodness.' (From The Book of Marco Polo.) Only thirty years after Genghis Khan's death, Persian and Chinese historians were writing in the same vein.

Genghis attacked Khorezm on the pretext that his ambassadors had been killed, for he always held that the rights of ambassadors should be recognised. A Sung general recounted this story of an ambassador at the Mongol court: 'One day Genghis asked the ambassador why he had not joined him and his friends in a game, and the ambassador replied that he had not dared as he had not been invited. Genghis said that the ambassador was a friend and should come on all the hunts and to all the feasts; he then burst out laughing, ordered music, beautiful women and wine, and only let the ambassador go when they had both got extremely drunk.'

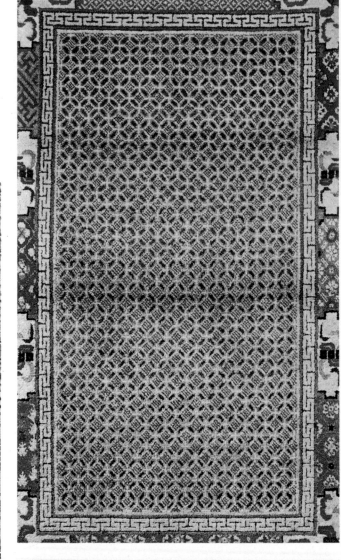

Above: a Mongolo-Tibetan carpet. Top right: Mongolo-Chinese carpet with decorations in gold. Bottom right: Mongolo-Chinese embroidery. Mongols have for many centuries been expert at embroidering, one of their outstanding designs being mosaic patterns in felt.

Opposite (left): carpet from Azerbaijan. (centre): Mongol carpet that was woven on a frame before the threads were knotted. (right): carpet made by nomadic Mongols who live between the Caucasus and Turkistan. Carpets were considered by the Mongols to be signs of nobility and power.

GENGHIS SEEKS A MEDICINE THAT GIVES ETERNAL LIFE

Now that the last resistance in Afghanistan had been crushed, the revolts in Persia put down and the people pacified, Genghis Khan proceeded to organise his new territories. He asked a Moslem sage if the holocaust at Merv would remain forever in people's minds, to which the wise man replied that there would be no Persians left to remember it if Genghis continued to persecute Moslems in this way. Genghis was angry at this reply and said that the Persian race was only one of many, and that his fame would nevertheless still spread throughout Islam even if he had to die in the process. But Genghis Khan was disturbed by this conversation, and so he began to try and find out more about the various religious beliefs of the people whom he had overrun and conquered. As a result, priests were exempted from taxation. This was as much as to say that killings were merely acts of war. He was sufficiently obsessed by this thirst for power to ask Chang Chun, a Taoist philosopher whom he had brought along with him from China, if there was any kind of medicine which would be able to give him eternal life.

The old man, of course, answered, much as one would have expected, namely that no such medicine existed. In the late summer of 1222 Genghis Khan camped in a pass of the Hindu Kush and there began planning new conquests. With these projects in mind, he sent messengers ahead, in order to see if they would be able to find a route across the Pamirs and Tibet. His messengers strongly advised against going in this direction, and so Genghis went back across the Amu-Dar'ya and spent the winter in Samarkand. The spring of 1223 saw him to the north of the Syr-Dar'ya and in March he fell off his horse while chasing a wild boar and very nearly died. He interpreted this as a warning from heaven and spent the following winter with Jagatai and Ogadei preparing for war before deciding to return home. He passed the summer of 1224 by the River Irtysh before finally reaching his homeland; waiting for him were Tului's sons, Kublai, who had conquered to the east, and Hulagu, who had conquered to the west. Genghis Khan's activities in Moslem countries were now at an end.

*Below: a Rumanian fresco of Turks
wearing turbans and Mongols
wearing pointed felt hats.
Right: a Christian city being
besieged by the Mongols (possibly
the siege of Constantinople). The
Mongols' first invasion of Europe
was followed by a second in the
course of which they reached the
Mediterranean.*

*Right: three wood-engravings from
Sebastian Münster's* Cosmographia
*(Basle 1552) of scenes of Mongol
life, the first two showing the
Mongols' interest in adventure and
hunting. The third engraving
illustrates the Mongols'
cannibalistic tendencies. In the
words of Joannes de Plan Carpini,
'The Mongols eat dogs, wolves,
foxes and even human flesh. If, after
a besieged city has surrendered,
there is not enough to eat, every
tenth prisoner is eaten.'*

THE MONGOL ARMY REACHES THE VOLGA

After the death of the Shah of Khorezm, Gebe and Subutai continued to conquer more and more land in the west. Azerbaijan and Kurdistan were defeated, and then, in February 1221, the Mongols met the Georgian army, which was just on the point of leaving for the conquest of Jerusalem under the command of their King, Giorgi III. This was the flower of the Georgian cavalry, and the most valiant army of the period, but ironically it was defeated and wiped out in a single ambush. After causing more devastation in the cities of western Persia, the Mongols returned to Georgia where they defeated yet another army. Then, braving bitter winds and freezing temperatures, they made the arduous crossing of the ice and the eternal snows of the Caucasus to the Caspian Pass, where, much to their surprise, they met a mighty army. This had been formed by the Alani, Lezgians, Circassians and Kumans who had perceived the imminent danger and had entered into an alliance with one another. Thanks to fine gifts and even more splendid promises of booty, the Mongols were able to persuade the Kumans, who were related to them, to fight on their side. The remainder of the opposing army was routed and the Mongols then set about annihilating the Kumans and taking back the presents they had given them. Some of the Kumans escaped to Greece where the Emperor of Byzantium gave them land in Thrace and Asia Minor, whilst others crossed the Prut and settled in Hungary. One of their generals, Kuthen, asked for help from his son-in-law, the Russian prince Mstislav of Galich. In answer to this call the princes of Kiev, Chernigov and Smolensk lined up their armies along the Dnieper. In the first skirmish, 80,000 well-armed Russians easily beat the tired Mongols who had only been able to muster some 20,000 men. They retreated to a bend of the Kalka and, on May 31st 1223, attacked each of the Russian armies in turn and defeated them. Then they sacked the Genoese trading posts of Sudak, in the Crimea, watered their horses in the Volga near what is now Volgograd, and went on to defeat the Turks from the Urals and the Bulgars. Throughout their journey of 4,000 miles the Mongols had left behind them a trail of destruction and fear, and they only returned home at this point because Genghis had announced a *quriltai*.

GENGHIS KHAN PREPARES FOR HIS LAST BATTLE

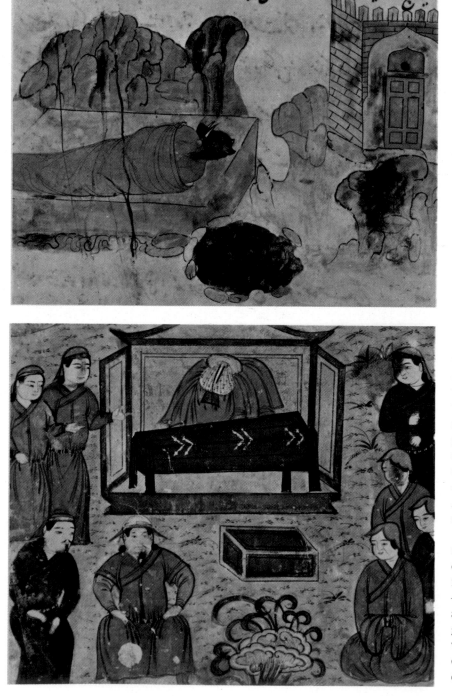

Genghis was hunting one autumn day on the slopes of Burkan Kaldun when he was so moved by the beauty of the countryside that he said to those accompanying him that this spot should be his burial place. To his close friends, in fact, this was interpreted as a premonition of his own death. On his return from his campaigns in the west, he announced that there was to be a meeting of all of his subjects, and this was also to include the Tanguts who came from the kingdom of Hsi Hsia. However, the king of the Tanguts wanted to demonstrate that he was the master of his own kingdom, and that he exercised authority over, and had the respect of, his own people. He, therefore, deliberately defied Genghis Khan by refusing to allow a detachment of his men to attend the meeting. The conquest of the whole of China was in fact made rather more difficult by the independence of Hsi Hsia, which lay to the north-west. In the autumn of 1226, therefore, Genghis marched on the Tanguts with an enormous army, whose strength has been estimated as no less than 180,000 men, and he also took with him one of his Tartar wives. One after another, the Hsi Hsia cities collapsed as they were attacked. The inhabitants were forced to flee for their lives from their own homes and sought refuge in mountains, ravines and caves, whilst the Mongols burnt their homes. But while his army was besieging Ning-sia, the capital of the Tangut kingdom, Genghis fell from his horse and seriously injured himself. Knowing that he was soon going to die, Genghis gave his last orders, planned his campaigns against southern China and chose as his successor Ogadei, in whom he could see some of his own qualities. At the same time he heard the news of Juchi's death. Genghis died on the fifteenth day of the second month in the Year of the Pig (August 18th, 1227). This was kept a close secret until Ning-sia surrendered, whereupon all the inhabitants were executed. Genghis' body was then carried on a cart for many miles – as was the custom among the nomads – to the foothills of Burkan Kaldun, and any man or animal met on the way was killed by the soldiers guarding the cortège. Also accompanying the cortège were Genghis Khan's five wives, his innumerable children and his 500 concubines, but to this day we do not know the exact whereabouts of the tomb.

Far left: a Chinese glazed painting of Burkan Kaldun.
Near left: a small votive pillar in Mongolia bearing the name of Genghis Khan. Below: a cave on Burkan Kaldun to which Mongols used to bring gifts, and probably where Genghis Khan's tomb was placed. The funerals of the great khans were grim occasions; according to Marco Polo, 'When dead princes were brought to Burkan Kaldun to be buried, the journey may last up to forty days and all who observe the cortège are killed so that they immediately go and serve their master in the next world . . . When Genghis died, more than 20,000 were killed in this way.'

Top: European miniature of
Mongols and Arabs fighting
(Oesterreichische Nationalbiblio-
thek, Vienna). Above: French
miniature showing Kublai's
expedition to Japan (The Book of
Marco Polo, Bibliothèque Nationale
Paris). Right: French miniature –
Kublai giving a pass known
as the 'golden tablet' to Marco
Polo and a fellow-Italian (The
Book of Marco Polo, Bibliothèque
Nationale, Paris). Marco
Polo reached Peking in 1275 and
stayed until 1292.

GENGHIS KHAN'S HEIRS AND THEIR CONQUESTS

Genghis had four sons by Burte and, according to Mongol tradition, each inherited one part of their father's domain, the eldest taking the area furthest from home and the youngest taking the area that included the home camp. This meant that Juchi controlled the west including Siberia and Turkistan, Jagatai the territory of the Khara Khitai, Ogadei the lands between Lake Balkhash and the Altai, and Tului Mongolia and most of the army. Ogadei conquered further provinces in the east and set up a capital at Karakorum, laying the foundations of an even greater empire. However, this vast scheme failed owing to internal dissension, although Ogadei retained his overall power from 1229 until his death in 1241. He was succeeded by his widow, Toragana, and in 1246 by his eldest son, Guyuk, who died in 1248 at a very early age, as the result of alcoholism. Guyuk's widow, Oghul Khaimish, was the Mongols' next leader but she was overthrown by Mangu, Tului's eldest son. Mangu had been aided in his coup by Batu, one of Juchi's sons; his reign (1251-1259) was one of relative peace and was highlighted by further victories in China, the conquest of Tibet and advances as far down as Annam. When he died his brother Kublai became emperor, in spite of claims by the legitimate heir Ariq Böge, and by certain princes in the west. He was nonetheless an exceptionally fine general, transferring the Mongol capital to Peking, conquering the whole of the rest of China and establishing the Yüan Dynasty (from *Ta Yüan* or 'Great Origin'). Kublai also built the 'Forbidden City' at Peking and, in the middle, a huge palace where Marco Polo was later to stay. He then marched through Korea and on to Japan (which he never succeeded in conquering, partly because his fleet was destroyed by a typhoon), Indo-China and Hava. Kublai's successors were considerably less successful; the most important of these was his son Temur, who reigned from 1294 until his death in 1307. The last of all his descendants to become emperor was Togon Temür, who did so on July 19th 1333 at the age of thirteen. He was deposed by a Chinese soldier of fortune who chased the Mongols out of China in a series of battles during the period 1355-1368. The Chinese soldier then helped to set up the Ming Dynasty.

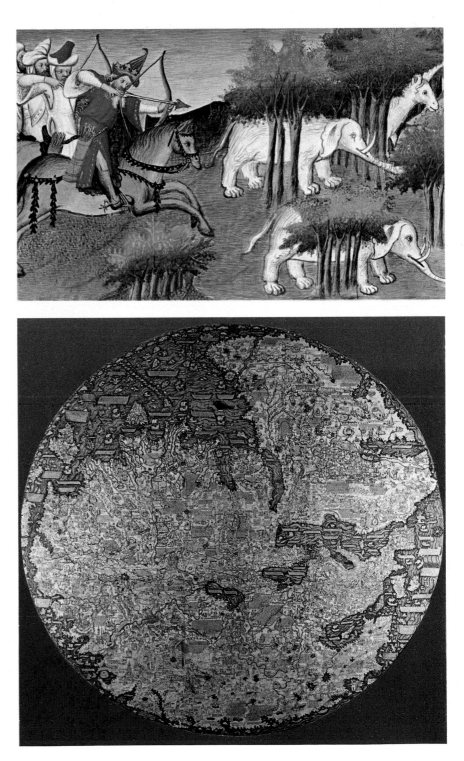

CERTAIN AREAS OF THE MONGOL EMPIRE DEVELOP SLOWLY

Below: an Il-khan ceramic panel for a tapestry, once in Hulagu's throne room. The technique and style are Persian but the dragon chasing the pearl is characteristic of the Yüan Dynasty. Even in Persia, Mongol artistic influence is to be found in the fusing of Persian techniques and designs, and Chinese styles of decoration.

Bottom: This Persian miniature shows Genghis listening to a story: 'The world is divided into five colours: the south is Red, the west is White, the east is Blue, the north is Black and the centre is Violet; the spirit of the Mongols has given Genghis Khan victory over all these colours and an ordu for every colour.'

The regions of Persia that had been conquered by the Mongols were ruled by a number of immensely powerful generals who expanded the territory to include such areas as Georgia and Asia Minor. For twenty years local chieftains had experienced a substantial amount of independence. However, in 1251, Mangu entrusted the territory to his younger brother, Hulagu, but only on condition that Genghis Khan's laws should be adopted everywhere from the Amu-Dar'ya to Egypt, and anyone who ignored these reforms should be executed. The centre of the Mongol Empire consisted of Jagatai's territories in the north and Hulagu's in the south. Prior to the Mongol invasion, Jagatai's lands had never been able to establish themselves as autonomous regions and they therefore remained the most traditional and, as a result, possibly the most backward part, of the whole empire. Most of the inhabitants were simple peasants, who built very few stone towns, preferring, instead, to organise raids and pillage the cities in the south of Khorezm, like Bukhara and Samarkand. They also created difficulties by being continually in open revolt against other territories of which Genghis Khan's successors were the overlords. On several occasions they attempted to conquer India by crossing the Hindu Kush and northern Afghanistan, and on one or two occasions they even managed to travel as far as Delhi. Jagatai reigned from the year 1227 to 1242 and was eventually succeeded, first by Hulagu, then by Organa (1252-1261) and Algu (1265-1266). Under the latter, Jagatai's lands were relatively free from interference and received from the central government a certain measure of independence which is best illustrated by the advance of Islam under the usurper, Baraq, some years later. This great empire was at its height in the 14th and 15th centuries, but in the early part of the 16th century it was split into the kingdoms of Tansoxiana and Mongolistan. This was a happy period of history for soldiers of fortune like Tughluq Timur, who had himself and 160,000 of his subjects converted to Islam on a single day, and Tamberlane. Later the empire was fragmented into smaller and smaller kingdoms which became so weak that they were eventually conquered by the Russians – Bukhara and Khiva being taken over as late as 1920 – and the last traces of Mongol power vanished.

Left: a Persian miniature which shows Persian craftsmen as prisoners (Bibliothèque Nationale, Paris). Below left: a feast given by Hulagu (Imperial Library, Tehran). Below right: an Il-khan miniature of animals painted in the Persian style against a background in the Chinese style. (University Library, Istanbul).

*Below left: a sixteenth-century
fresco of Constantine the Great,
painted in thanksgiving for the
expulsion of the Mongols (A mon-
astery in Kremkovtsi, Bulgaria).
Below right: a Russian helmet
made in the Mongolo-Persian style
(Kremlin Museum, Moscow).
Bottom: King Ladislaw of Rumania
fighting the Kumans.*

*Right: Saints Boris and Gleb, the
sons of St Wladimir and patron
saints of the soldiers who fought the
Mongols in the 13th century (State
Gallery, Leningrad).
Facing page (left): King Kaloyan
of Bulgaria and his wife.
(right): Tsar Constantine Asen
and his wife (Church of a small
town near Sofia).*

MONGOL HORDES REACH THE ADRIATIC

When Subutai informed the Russians that he did not want to go to war with them, he sent ten envoys but these, unfortunately, were killed. He then sent two more along with the message: 'You murdered our envoys and attacked our outposts without warning. Do you want war? We have done you no harm. Let God be the judge.'

Genghis Khan's eldest son, Juchi, would automatically have inherited the kingdoms of the west if he had not died before his father. As it was, his son Batu set off in the footsteps of Gebe and Subutai in 1238 and conquered the lands to the north of the Black Sea before devastating Kiev and Ruthenia. He then divided his army, which probably numbered 150,000 men, into two parts, sending one against Boleslaw, King of Poland, who was defeated at Chmielnik on March 18th, 1241. On April 9th of the same year, the remainder of Batu's forces massacred an army composed of Germans and Poles under the command of Henry II the Pious of Silesia at the Battle of Legnica (Liegnitz). Meanwhile another Mongol army under Qaidu was defeating Wenceslas, King of Bohemia, who died on the battlefield. After defeating the Hungarians under Bishop Ugolin, a combined Mongol army led by Subutai wiped out a force of Magyars, Croats, Germans and French Templars under King Béla showing a strategic skill reminiscent of Genghis Khan himself. In July 1241 the Mongols were within striking distance of Vienna, and that winter Batu crossed the frozen Danube and took Graz while another army went down the Adriatic plundering the towns of Split and Udine. Just about this time Ogadei died in Mongolia and on January 4th 1242 it was decided to convoke a *quriltai*. Batu was one of those ordered to go back home and so Europe was saved further destruction. The enormous territory conquered by Batu stretched from Lake Aral to the Dnestr, but much of it was slowly won back by Ivan the Terrible (1530-1584), Tsar of Muscovy. Ivan was helped in this by the breaking-up of the territory into smaller kingdoms. The most important of these kingdoms was that of the Kalmyks who overran the Russian principality of Kazan and then, in 1643, settled between the Volga and the Don, occasionally raiding the Mongol kingdoms in Siberia. They allied themselves with Peter the Great, but finally left Russian territory and returned to central Asia. As late as 1720 the Dzungars pushed Russian troops back to Lake Zaisan but Peter the Great soon occupied most of the territories belonging to the Mongols in Russia. The last Mongol lands – in the Crimea – fell in 1783.

Below: this is a lustre ceramic plate which was made in Persia in the 13th century, and it is decorated with pictures of Mongol warriors.
Bottom left: a photograph of copper container which is meant to hold either opium or hashish.
Bottom right: a narghile which was made from coco palm. It was discovered in a Mongol fortress. Marco Polo wrote at some length of the Old Men of the Mountains and even the young men who imagined they were in Paradise after taking opium or hashish. From hashshashin, *the Arabic word for people who take hashish, is derived the English word 'assassin.'*

Hulagu's first act in Persia was to put an end to the marauding activities of a powerful Ishmaelite sect. Their 'fortresses' at Mazanderan and Alamut were so inaccessible that they closely resembled eagles' nests. However, an army left the new Mongol capital of Tabriz and wiped out all the enemy strongholds one by one, under the personal supervision of Hulagu himself; the leader of this Ishmaelite sect died in chains on his way to Mongolia. Then Hulagu, a fervent Buddhist, decided to attack Baghdad, the spiritual capital of Mahommedanism. After an exchange of threatening letters, Hulagu entered the city in November 1257 and met with scarcely any resistance – due to the fact that the Caliph had no army. On February 10th 1258 and for the next two days, 90,000 inhabitants were put to death, and then the city was sacked for seventeen days and finally set on fire. At the intercession of Hulagu's Nestorian wife, the Christians were spared and later given high administrative posts. The Caliph's treasure was taken to an island on Lake Urmia in Azerbaijan, and then Hulagu joined with King Hethum I of Armenia and Bohemund VI of Antioch with the purpose of attacking the Syrian Ayyubids. After a number of swift victories, Aleppo and Damascus fell in February 1260 and the Syrian Jacobites acclaimed Hulagu and his wife as 'the new Constantine and Helen'. The Mongols had reached Samaria and were marching on Egypt when the news of Mangu's death (August 11th 1259), and of the warring claimants to the succession, sent Hulagu back to Mongolia. This respite gave the Mamelukes in Egypt time to re-arm and in 1260 they succeeded in forcing the Mongols out of Palestine and Syria. On his death in 1265, Hulagu was succeeded by his son who was remorselessly attacked by the tribes from lands once ruled by Jagatai and then by the Mamelukes, and was from time to time defeated by the latter. His place was taken in 1282 by another of Hulagu's sons who became a Mahommedan and was forcibly ejected by his grandson in 1284. The throne was occupied in the early 14th century by a number of only moderately successful princes, including Ghazan. The last of them was Abu Sa'id, the only khan to have an Arabic name, and there then followed a period of anarchy, of which Tamberlane was quick to take advantage.

Left: this is a resting-place on the road from Kayseri to Siyas which was built by the Turks between the years 1229 and 1236; it is similar in some ways to resting-places on Mongol roads. The Mongols were rather backward compared with the Turks but they soon adapted themselves to the ways of civilisation.

Below: an embroidery of a Mongol scene, which was made in the Middle East, towards the end of the 19th century, according to a technique which followed very closely that which was employed by Mongol craftsmen in Genghis Khan's time. Recent studies have underlined the influence of Mongol art on Europe and the rest of Asia.

Below: decorated window of Akbar's mausoleum in India, in the Indo-Islamic style of the Moguls. Top right: mausoleum at Agra, a fine example of Indo-Islamic art at the time of the Moguls in India. Bottom right: lapwing made of steel at the time of Tamberlane. Facing page: a Timurid miniature of a hunting party.

Under Tamberlane, Persia saw the beginning of a cultural revival, and the Timurid period corresponds to the Renaissance in Europe. In addition to the examples quoted in this book, important works of this period include Tamberlane's mausoleum, which is somewhat in the shape of a tent and is entirely covered with polychrome ceramics, and a bronze cauldron made by Tamberlane in Samarkand and weighing two tons – the heaviest piece of metalwork in Moslem art. Timurid craftsmen also excelled in the fashioning of steel and in the painting of miniatures, but probably the great glory of Moslem art is its architecture, and of this the finest examples are probably those at Agra.

TAMBERLANE

Tamberlane – Timur i Leng (Timur the lame) – was born on April 8th 1336 at Kesh (modern Shakhrisyabz), which was fifty miles south of Samarkand. He was a Turk, not a Mongol, and in the beginning was an insignificant chieftain of the Barlas clan. Styling himself a 'direct descendant' of Genghis Khan, he firstly proved his loyalty to his king, Tughlaq Temür, a successor to Jagatai. However in 1361 he himself replaced an uncle as governor of Kesh and took over the government of Transoxiana by defeating one of his allies, Ilyas Khoja, with the help of Amir Husain, King of Kabul. After having Amir Husain assassinated, he conquered Balkh and proclaimed himself king in the year 1370. From 1372 to 1390, Tamberlane carried out a series of military campaigns against the usurpers of Mongolistan, was able to restore the legitimate heir to the throne, and swept through Mesopotamia, Armenia and Georgia, leaving piles of heads at the gates of any city that resisted him. He helped Tokhtamysh to become Khan of the White Horde so that he could defeat the Golden Horde, but immediately afterwards he turned against his ally and took from him Azerbaijan, the Crimea and Ciscausi. By the end of the 14th century, Tamberlane's territory had been extended as far south as Delhi, and in 1400 and 1401 he conquered Aleppo and Damascus. After this he proceeded to overthrow the Ottoman Bayazid I, and at Smyrna massacred the Knights of the Hospital of St John of Jerusalem. It had originally been his intention to invade China and give it a Moslem civilisation, but he was wounded at Otrar and died there on January 19th, 1405. Until 1507, when they were wiped out by the Uzbek Mohammed Khan Shaibani, his descendants were all outstanding warriors: Babut (the Tiger), whose mother was a direct descendant of Genghis Khan, having been driven out of his lands in Fergana and Samarkand by the Uzbeks, reached Delhi and there, in 1526, founded one of the most famous empires in the world – the Mogul Empire; and Akbar, under whom the Mogul Empire eventually comprised almost the whole of India. Under Akbar's successors, however, the empire gradually passed into European hands until the last of the Mogul Emperors, Bahadur Shah II, handed over the empire to the British on December 8th, 1858.

The warlike fervour of the Mongols did not lose its impetus with the death of Genghis, for in the next twenty years much of the rest of Asia was conquered by his sons and grandsons; the world seemed theirs for the asking. Then the deaths of Ogadei and Mangu put an end to the campaigns in Europe and the western tip of Asia respectively and the Mongol empire was actually stabilised by the evacuation from Syria and Yugoslavia. But, as a result of quarrels, and claims by various tribes for independence, the empire began to crumble. Of the vast edifice built up by a single man and all that remains today are ruined cities, memories – and a nation.

MODERN MONGOLIA IS ALL THAT REMAINS OF GENGHIS KHAN'S EMPIRE

Genghis Khan died about 700 years ago and all that remains of his vast empire is the young Republic of Mongolia. The nomads, who live there, still look after their flocks and herds in a similar manner to that of their predecessors, fight one another with bows and arrows and live in the same sort of circular, felt tents that their forefathers used. The great plains are still covered with ice in winter and are baked dry when the temperature soars in the summer, and in the spring miles and miles of flowers appear in this harsh and yet beautiful land. Nothing, it appears, has changed and it is even said that some tribes go up to the summit of a mountain once a year and there offer up fermented milk to the spirit of the dead Genghis Khan. Until quite recent times the Shamans used to be in the habit of leaving offerings four times a year at Genghis Khan's sanctuary, which is to be found on the Ordos plateau. Old men recount stories of the last kingdoms of Astrakhan, Kokand (which itself became incorporated into Russia in 1876), Bukhara and Khiva. And there are still numerous songs about the stirring events which occurred during the years of the last great Mongol empire – about Toghon and his son Esen Taiji, and of the Dzungars, who were China's most feared enemy in the 17th and 18th centuries. Mongol influence dwindled over the centuries, however, and between 1686 and 1911 Mongolia was governed by the Manchu emperors. The sudden revolution in China in 1911 gave much encouragement to the Mongolian separatist movement and on March 31st, 1921 Mongolia managed to achieve independence with the assistance of Russian military aid. On November 26th, 1924 the government proclaimed the Mongolian People's Republic, which was to enter into an alliance with the Soviet Union in 1945. Mongolia covers an area of about 615,000 square miles, though once the Mongols marched distances that could more easily be measured in degrees of latitude and longitude than in miles. The average height of this extensive steppe plateau is about 4000 feet, although the highest mountain peak, which is the Tabun Boydo, reaches 15,266 feet. Mongolia is bordered by the Soviet Union in the north and China in south, east and west. To the south is the Great Wall of China. Within these limits the once-mighty Mongol peoples are contained.

Facing page (top): a tent identical to those occupied by Genghis and his warriors; only the motor-cycle is anachronistic. (bottom): sheep grazing on a Mongolian plain. Left: shepherd wearing clothes identical to those described by Marco Polo in 1299. Below: nomads in Karakorum. Bottom: a woman in Ulan Bator.

Below: a Timurid painting of the Shiraz school showing Genghis during his conquest of China (British Museum, London). The best accounts of Genghis Khan's life were written and illustrated in Persia at the time of the Il-khans and Timurids, but the earliest sources are Mongol and Chinese: Mongghol-un ni'usha tobsh'an (The secret history of the Mongols) by an unknown author and written in either 1240 or 1252; Huang Yuan sheng-wu ts'in (1263), the Chinese translation of a lost Mongol text; and Yuan-she, a Chinese book written in 1369-1370. There are two important Persian works: Ta'rikh-i-Jahan-Gusha (History of the World-Conqueror) by 'Ala ud-Din 'Ata-Malik Juvaini and Jami al-tawarikh (History of the World) by Rashid ed-Din, both written during the Il-khan period. Further information can be found in The Book of Marco Polo, History of the Mongols by H. Howorth and The Rise of Chingis Khan and His Conquest of Northern China by H. D. Martin.

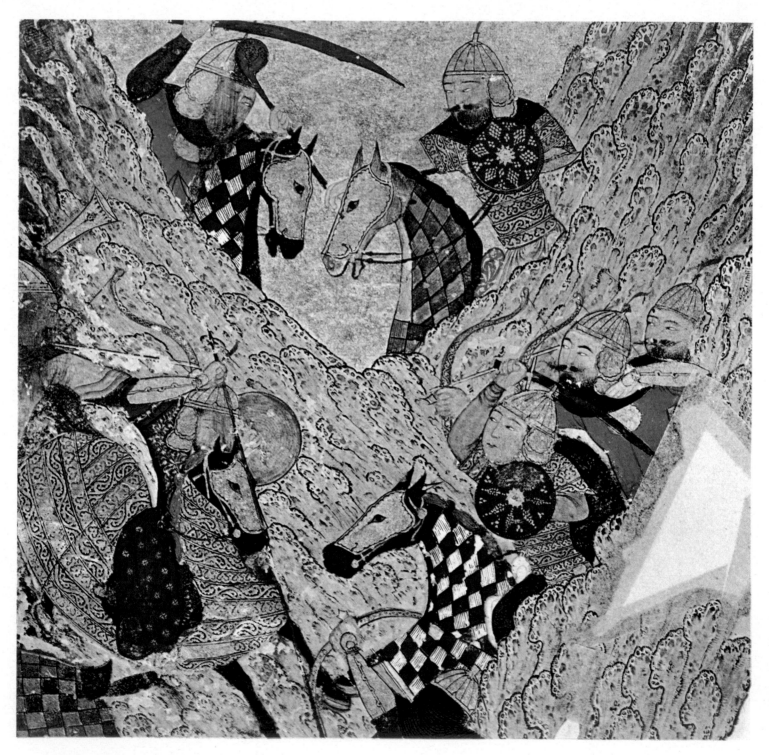

Genghis Khan started his campaign for the domination of the world with eight horses and four brothers. In his lifetime, he was able to unite disparate peoples that otherwise would only have remained enemies, and he was the leader of the largest and the richest empire the world has ever known. His greatest virtues were an ability to sum up an intricate and difficult situation immediately, the courage to take decisions quickly and an intuitive military skill which enabled him to turn apparent defeat into glorious victory. He prepared for battles in great detail, although he was unable either to read or to write, he directed the complicated movements of his troops without taking part in the fighting himself and he outwitted the most experienced and shrewdest of opposing generals. In his lifetime he was able to build up an empire that easily survived him, and it was an empire that was based on the magnanimous laws that he had set down, and even today the Mongolian is known for his loyalty, morality and honesty. No warrior or politician has achieved so much, particularly with such uneducated and unorganised people. He was surrounded by conspiracies and human suffering, and, no doubt, at the end of his life he could have been admired and venerated as a god if he had so desired. However he considered himself merely as God's representative and prophet.

1155 – (according to Islamic sources); **1162** – (according to Chinese sources); **1176** – (according to European scholarship) – Temujin born.
1201 – Attacked by Jamukha, defeats him, annexes his pasture grounds.
1203 – Obliged by Toghril to flee; returns, defeats him and annexes his territory.
1206 – The various Mongol tribes recognise Temujin as their leader and proclaim him Genghis Khan.
1207 – Annexes the Oirates, the Kirgiz and the Uighurs.
1209 – Marches into the Tangut kingdom of Hsi Hsia.
1211 – A hostile relationship develops between Genghis and the Kin Empire.
1215 – Peking surrenders.
1219 – The Mongols march west; Moslem states, large and small, are wiped out.
1220 – Bukhara and Samarkand fall.
1221 – Afghanistan conquered.
1222 – Gebe and Subutai reach the Volga and the Crimea.
1223 – The Russians suffer their first defeat near the River Kalka.
1225 – Genghis returns to Mongolia.
1226 – Genghis attacks the kingdom of Hsi Hsia.
1227 – Genghis dies near Ningsia, the capital of Hsi Hsia, which surrenders shortly afterwards; his body is carried back to Mongolia.
1229 – Genghis Khan's third son, Ogadei, is elected leader and finally conquers the Kin Empire, Persia and southern Russia (the area near the Caspian Sea and the mouth of the

Volga).
1241 – Mongol forces invade Hungary and Poland; Battle of Chmielnik (March 18th); Polish and German army routed at the Battle of Legnica (April 9th); Béla IV pushed back to the Adriatic; Mongol advances halted by the news of Ogadei's death (December 11th); Batu, Genghis Khan's grandson and commander of the Mongol forces in Europe, returns to Karakorum for the election of the new khan; a group of Mongols returning home found the city of Sarai on the lower Volga.
1241–1246 – Interregnum.
1245–1247 – Joannes de Plan Carpini in Mongolia at the request of Pope Innocent IV and writes his impressions in *Historia mongolorum*.
1246–1248 – The reign of Guyuk, Ogadei's son; on his death, power passes into the hands of the children of Tului, Genghis Khan's fourth son.
1250 – Death of Emperor Frederick II who, after the invasions of Hungary and Poland, pleaded in vain with other European monarchs to repel the Mongol insurgents.
1251–1259 – The reign of Mangu.
1260 – An Arab army under the Mameluke Sultan al-Muzaffar Sayf al-Din Qutuz defeats the Mongols under Hulagu who had advanced as far as Syria (Battle of Ayn Jalut, September 3rd); When Mongol forces are routed a few years later by another Mameluke Sultan, Mongol aspirations of dominating the Mediterranean die.
1260–1294 – The reign of Kub-

lai, Tului's second son, who succeeded Mangu; under him, Genghis Khan's people cease to be nomadic and begin to feel the influence of Chinese culture; Kublai moves his capital to Peking and founds the Yüan Dynasty.
1275–1295 – Marco Polo stays at Kublai's court.
1336 – Tamberlane born in Samarkand.
1368 – The Mongols are defeated by armies of the Ming Dynasty.
1400–1401 – Tamberlane leads the Mongols to Damascus.
1405 – Tamberlane dies while preparing to invade China.
1526 – Babur founds the Empire of the Grand Moguls in Delhi.
1550–1584 – Ivan the Terrible drives most of the Mongols out of Russia.
1686–1911 – Mongolia occupied by the Manchu.
1783 – The last remaining Mongol outpost – in the Crimea – is wiped out by the Russians.
1858 – The last of the Grand Moguls, Bahadur Shah, is deposed by the British.
1876 – The Mongol territories of Astrakhan and Kokand are occupied by the Russians.
1911 – The Mongolian separatist movement becomes active.
1920 – The Mongol strongholds of Bukhara and Khiva are conquered by the Russians.
1921 – Constitution of an autonomous Mongolian state proclaimed (March 31st).
1924 – The Mongolian People's Republic proclaimed.
1945 – Friendly alliance signed with the Soviet Union.

The works reproduced in this book are preserved in the following collections. Berlin, Museum für Völkerkunde: p.10. Kabul, private collection: pp. 20, 55. Florence, private collection: p. 37. Galenzia Cathedral, Transylvania: p. 66. Istanbul, University Library: pp. 28-29. Institute of Islamic and Oriental Archaeology (Italy): p. 37, 51. British Museum: p. 47, 53, 74. Milan, Civica Raccolta Stampe Bertarelli: frontispiece, pp. 39, 58-9. Eskenazi Collection: p. 11. Milan, Museo Poldi Pezzoli: p. 47. Moscow, Kremlin Imperial Treasures: p. 66. Paris, Bibliothèque Nationale: 12, 15, 25, 26, 27, 29, 31, 36, 42, 45, 60, 62, 63, 64, 65. Paris, Musée des Arts-Decoratifs: p. 44. Parma, Museo d'Arte Cinese: p 24. Peshawar Museum: p. 6. Seattle Art Museum: p. 55. Sofia, church of Bojana: p. 67. Teheran, Imperial Library: pp. 17, 18-19, 30, 34, 54, 65, 71. Karmili Collection: p. 65. Venice, Biblioteca Marciana: p. 63. Vienna, Kunsthistorische Museum: p. 6. Oesterreichische Nat. Bibliothek: p. 62. Zagabria, private collection: p. 40. Photographic credits: Mondadori Photographic Archives: pp. 62, 63. Freeman: pp. 47, 53, 74. Magnum: pp. 72, 73. Guido Bianchi: p. 9. Gabriele Mandel was responsible for the collection and execution of the rest of the material.